Reflections

on

Higher

Education

STEPHEN JOEL TRACHTENBERG

ORYX PRESS

OTHER BOOKS BY STEPHEN JOEL TRACHTENBERG

Thinking Out Loud:
10 Years of Commentaries on Higher Education
(American Council on Education/Oryx Press, 1998)

Speaking His Mind:
5 Years of Commentaries on Higher Education
(American Council on Education/Oryx Press, 1994)

The Art of Hiring in America's Colleges & Universities
(Prometheus Books, 1993)

Library of Congress Cataloging-in-Publication Data available upon request.
Copyright © 2002
Stephen Joel Trachtenberg

Published by The Oryx Press
88 Post Road West
Westport, CT 06881

An imprint of Greenwood Publishing Group, Inc.
www.oryxpress.com

Library of Congress Catalog Card Number
ISBN: 1-57356-571-7

Published simultaneously in Canada

Printed and Bound in the United States of America

The paper used in this publication meets the minimum requirements of
American National Standard for Information Science—Permanence of Paper
for Printed Library Materials, ANSI Z39.48, 1984.

"The United States in the 21st Century" is reprinted
with permission from The World & I, November 2001.

"Great Expectations" is reprinted with permission from
The Presidency, Fall 2001, American Council on Education.

CONTENTS

This book is dedicated with the deepest appreciation and gratitude to Helene Interlandi, my assistant of 23 years, and to the members of The George Washington University Class of 2006.

Introduction

MANY YEARS AFTER he had published *A Tale of a Tub*, Jonathan Swift read it over and exclaimed, "What a genius I had when I wrote that book!" As I reviewed the speeches I have given in the last three years, I confess that I was not moved to a similar exclamation. While reading a few of them, I made a note to remind myself that sometimes silence is golden. In most cases, however, I was pleased with what I had to say and how I said it, but the observations I made on those occasions — like some very good wines — just wouldn't travel, and so they are not included here. There were some speeches I thought had some endurance and continuing interest, and the speeches in this collection come from that batch.

Those speeches, indeed like the others, were given to small and fairly specialized audiences — a group of experts in educational testing, for example, a Rotary Club, a seminar on leadership and management. But if I truly believed they still had something to say to a broader audience, then I thought it would be reasonable to collect several of them, edit them so they play a bit better to the eye of a reader than to the ear of a listener, and offer them to all comers. Hence, this little book.

As I looked over the speeches I had selected, it was obvious that, with two exceptions, they had a common theme — higher education in at least one of its incarnations or functions — and even the exceptions deal with public education or with education in general as a partial solution to the problem at hand. But something else caught me unaware — specifically, and just as obviously, a second theme I had not consciously intended. That theme is the differences between then and now or, to put it bluntly, change. Life and learning in the academy and elsewhere in our society are not what they used to be and in some cases not what we had in mind or ever could have imagined.

The fact that things change is not news. Twenty-five hundred years ago, Heraclitus taught us that only change itself is constant. But the changes that happen *to us* and somehow alter our lives — for better or worse, no matter — *are* news, at least to us. They ultimately may become parts of history, which is really the long record of change. But changes take digesting, and I suppose that's why I find myself — unconsciously, as I say — frequently ruminating on change.

Some of it is a function of age. Having turned my back on 60, it is natural, if not always easy to bear, that more and more of the things I thought good or eternal or simply the way things were and always would be are no longer considered good, eternal, or the way things are now. But that is one of the ancient themes of aging, sometimes called a longing for the good old days. What I think is different for people of my era is that the rate of change has accelerated in our lifetimes. How many people owned cars or their own homes 60 years ago? How many had telephones? Very few, yet today about two-thirds of Americans own their own homes (sometimes more than one), some 90 percent of American households have at least one car, well more than half have a computer, and there are virtually no households without a phone, not to mention a fax and a cell phone and a television, all of which have the habit of bringing new events to our doorsteps almost daily.

These modernizations reflect both material and cultural changes. And they have their consequences and parallels in the world of education. In the course of 60 years, college has grown from a rare opportunity, generally reserved for the well-to-do, to a middle-class entitlement. We are teaching courses and offering programs — many

splendid and some, I admit, less than necessary — that no one ever would have imagined 60 years ago. Yet there is a demand for them.

And I use the word *demand* in the sense economists use it. It reflects a market. How many university presidents 60 years ago, or even 20, would have ever thought — let alone openly talked — about an *education market* and their own school's share in it? None that I know of. Yet education exists in a marketplace, precisely because there is a demand for it and competition to meet the demand. In addition to producing innovation and better teaching, this may also produce redundancy and some second-rate schools and instruction, but markets are messy, as economists never fail to remind us. They also are, if only in the long run, efficient. Anyway, I accept this fact of academic life because it is impossible not to accept it. It is there.

It is for the same reason, I believe, that I noticed other recurrent themes in this collection of speeches. It would have been easy enough to edit them out or downplay them, but I thought it was worth the risk of being repetitious to reveal a university president's preoccupations.

The first is money. I can't help it: my university is many things, and one of them is a business. With an annual budget of about three-quarters of a billion dollars, but without a generous state legislature or an endowment like Harvard's, money is a preoccupation; even wealthy Harvard and Princeton spend a great deal of time and effort, including the time and effort of their presidents, on fund raising. To advance learning and service takes money. To provide the many different things the members of the university want, or need, or demand takes money. We might be considering more books in the library, a new building, a better intranet, the basketball team, flower gardens, higher salaries, improved garbage collection, or more scholarships, among many other possibilities. Not one of them is free. But I think the many different things people want *do* contribute to advancing learning and service, and so I set about getting the money. And, of course, thinking about it.

  Other recurring themes are intertwined. I refer several times to the "pervasiveness" of education in America, and I talk about something I call "The University of the United States," which represents the informal, but highly integrated, system of American higher education. Related to this is my repeated faith that the overall system of American higher education is the finest in the world. These, too, are preoccupations of mine and sources of immense optimism for me. I hope they are for other university presidents and for anyone concerned with higher education in America, including the readers of this book.

The

New

Millennium

The United States in the 21st Century

AS IT ENTERS the third millennium, the United States — while on its way to becoming a nation of 300 million people — has grown used to hearing itself described as the world's only remaining superpower. The role that such status brings with it — the role of being the world's policeman — is one with which the citizens of the United States are presently wrestling. Americans are deeply divided as to whether a role requiring global interventions of every imaginable kind is one that even a country as powerful as the United States can play.

Inner division of this sort becomes apparent each time there is a world emergency of some kind — especially when the emergency involves refugees or violations of human rights in a distant and preferably "primitive" setting. Only hours are needed, it seems, before those demanding immediate intervention by the American armed forces confront fellow Americans with the opposite point of view: those who are convinced that intervention is a symptom of moral and national decline.

Emergencies of this kind summon up, in a powerful way, several different strands of the American national character and history:

Reprinted with permission from *The World & I*, November 2001

- The desire to serve the world as a force of enlightenment and righteousness.

The cynicism induced by the wars of the 20th century — World Wars I and II, the Cold War, the Korean War, the Vietnam War, the Gulf War — has veiled but not eliminated the emotional conviction that America has been destined by God Himself to serve as a global savior. Such feelings have flowed into historical phenomena as varied as abolitionism (the ideological war against slavery), prohibition (the war against alcohol), and all the "reform" efforts that have created modern trade unionism, citizens' groups crusading on behalf of our natural environment, and all kinds of groups seeking to further humanitarian and peacemaking causes in a host of foreign countries.

- The conviction that the American sense of human rights, as incorporated in the first 10 amendments to the U.S. Constitution, is destined for acceptance by the entire human species.

One has to return to ancient Rome or to baroque Spain and France to discover such gut feelings of a God-given destiny. Americans have always been averse to thundering displays of military power such as were commonplace in Hitler's Germany or Stalin's Soviet Union. This does not lead them, however, to feel anything other than righteous indignation when a foreign regime displays obnoxious and aggressive military tendencies. When misbehavior becomes a habit in some foreign setting, Americans move reflexively into the position that "there must be *something* we can do." It may be enough for the American delegate to protest at the United Nations. Or sentiment may reach a higher pitch and nudge the American president toward actual, physical war.

- The sense of utopian perfectibility.

Americans often marvel at the fact that there are people in other nations who don't see themselves as being on a "march to perfection." Meanwhile, many foreigners find the United States an exhausting place to live because every American —

every businessperson, every government employee, every academician, and so forth — seems dedicated to doing his job even better. The notion that life is a quest for perfection can be traced back to some of the Protestant sects of the 17th and 18th centuries, who, in their own time, were called "Enthusiasts." For an American, to be glowing with a divine radiance while one is "advertising" one's product is just "the obvious way to be."

As Alexis de Tocqueville noted long ago, Americans never tire of forming voluntary citizens' associations aiming to make ours a better world. The spirit of this effort, as of so much of American life, is religious and evangelistic. No nation in history has ever spent as much time, effort, and money to toot its own horn as has the nation called the United States. Giant effigies of American presidents are carved into mountains. Along the Mall in Washington that runs from the Washington Monument to the Capitol, some of the world's greatest museums pay homage to the American spirit as one at least as good as the spirits of Europe and Asia.

Cynics have observed more than once that every nation is doomed to proving that its critics are wrong. So it is less than surprising that Americans are still engaged in disproving the criticisms of democracy leveled 200 years ago in Europe and 3,500 years ago in the Athens of Plato. Do those living in a democracy find themselves accused of being culturally deprived specimens whose notions of art begin with the comic pages of their daily newspapers? Then, of course, every American city must have its own unique museum, stuffed from the basement to the attic with masterpieces. Being so hopelessly devoted to equality, can Americans ever become truly great military figures? In that case, America of course produces figures like Ulysses S. Grant and George S. Patton, who either transform the art of modern warfare or posture in front of the cameras like a modern-day Alexander the Great or Oliver Cromwell. American schoolchildren aren't learning as much, and as quickly, as those in Copenhagen or Singapore? Then the president himself will promise a complete reform of American education — which seeks to

train tens of millions of children, most of them through school systems controlled by their local municipalities.

Americans, in short, represent a nation that has never stopped proving things — most of them having to do with issues of power or issues of aesthetics and wisdom. Natural results of these emotions include the social and cultural behaviors that so much of our world regards as questionable. By the traditional standards once maintained by the European upper class, one ought not to boast too vigorously of one's national achievements. However, to ask an American not to do this is like asking him not to cheer when his child scores a winning basket while playing with a school team. Americans are all too prone to suspect that they are not perfect enough. They are driven by emotions that once dominated the Reformation of Martin Luther and John Calvin — a period when many elements that would later form the American character were shaped.

AMERICAN COLLEGES AND UNIVERSITIES

Even Americans often lose sight of the extent to which their thoughts and feelings are now being molded by America's colleges and universities — of which there are now close to 3,000. Since Americans sharply limit the size and power of their federal government, no national model of either a college or a university has ever been developed. Instead, the 50 American states and the District of Columbia have set their own academic standards — while admittedly keeping a sharp eye on what the folks across the border are doing. The result has been a network of higher education, the policies of whose individual schools are remarkably uniform. Every school of higher education in the United States can understand, and award appropriate credit for, the student records it receives from any other school. It is no longer unusual for one student to attend four or five different schools before receiving a degree — typically a B.A. or an M.A. — from one of them.

This loose but uniform system of higher education helps to explain why more than 60 percent of all Americans have experienced

at least some college. This has changed the United States in only one or two generations from a land dominated by its blue-collar workers — its unskilled laborers — to one where political and economic power is synonymous with academic degrees. (It is symbolic of these changes that George W. Bush is the first American president to hold an M.B.A. — a master's of business administration.)

Thus, higher education has to imply an important American glue or cement. Increasingly, it holds America together by shaping the values and passions of the average American citizen. Those who work in higher education are used to hearing, in their colleges or universities, a note of missionary zeal that is rarely heard in communities other than Australia or New Zealand, where educators must deal with minority populations long ignored or mistreated by their nations' higher education systems. The missionary note, in the United States, is especially strong where the colleges of the center-cities are concerned. These colleges in the center-cities struggle to combine their commitment to excellence with their commitment to American society. Often, they consciously transfer funds from programs that merely benefit the intellectually superior to programs with greater outreach and greater amounts of ethnic diversity.

AMERICA AS AN EXPERIMENT

But even the above does not fully capture a unifying characteristic of the United States. There is a growing consensus to the effect that America is an experiment, perhaps an experiment by God, perhaps an experiment of the human mind, but an experiment of some sort. There were some who reflected this thought from the earliest days of the Republic. George Washington makes mention of the notion in his inaugural address, and Jefferson referred to it in both of his inaugural addresses as well. Nevertheless, one doesn't sense that it was broadly felt in the 18th and 19th centuries. It has depended on the great "triumph of science," from Darwin and Einstein to Jonas Salk, Isidor Rabi, and the researchers of every major university. To describe America as a conscious "experiment" no longer arouses the feelings that it might have sparked a century or two ago.

Like some of the thought patterns outlined above, the notion of America as an experiment also has a concealed purpose. It enables Americans to hold on to the feeling that they are unique among the nations of our planet — that they, and they alone, have brought modern wisdom to bear on their daily behaviors.

I have placed much emphasis on the ideological bases of today's America instead of on statistics of its industrial growth or agricultural production. This is because Americans so often insist that they are not driven by bad old habits like ideology or religion. As the world's anthropologists noted many years ago, cultures often incorporated rituals of denial into their most cherished habits — like the ancient Romans who awarded Caesar his triumph while seeing to it that a special servant whispered in his ear: "Remember that you are mortal."

Americans are no exception. They resent ideology for the same reason that their Constitution abhors tyrants. Ideology is seen as consisting, typically, of some mad manifesto perpetrated by a Napoleon or a Hitler. This is why in the 1960s, when "radicals" insisted that even one's clothing or style of walking could reflect membership in the "ruling class," most Americans responded with completely deaf ears. To do otherwise, they would have had to admit that, of course, Americans spent half their time denying what they spent the other half of their lives affirming and perpetrating.

Which brings me to the highly important subject of Americans and the media. Much of the world has always been stunned by the speed, the virtual instantaneity, with which Americans have developed their technology and electronic ways of staying in touch with each other. Shortwave radios had no sooner become an expensive treasure than Americans were broadcasting "all the news, all the time" from every corner of our planet to radios, many of them in automobiles, that cost a trifle. From the time when a television set was likely to be the only one on its block to the moment when every household had at least one or two, mere historical "seconds" seemed to elapse. In one year, Hollywood was just starting to develop. A few years later, it was already the entertainment capital of the world.

There are different ways of accounting for this media passion. One is to point to the size of America. For persons so widely spread to stay in touch with each other and with their common purposes, the argument runs, media like the telegraph, radio, and television had to be invented. Another argument points to the risky feeling one gets in a country made up of so many different ethnic and language groups. Many times in the 20th century, the new media were characterized as a force binding the huge nation together. They were often hailed for teaching English to those who would otherwise have difficulty functioning as full citizens.

But America's passion for the media, which so often drives the media penetration of the rest of the world, has another important root. This passion can be described as one natural consequence of a longstanding American concern — bringing the world under symbolic control.

Americans, as all the world knows, are especially devoted to stories based on the cowboys of the 19th century. Historians know that such cowboys, to the extent that they existed at all, mainly lived from about 1860 to 1880. They were thus only a flicker on the American struggle between ideals of expansion and ideals of control. The characters in American westerns are typically persons dealing with exactly this struggle.

ENERGETIC SETTLEMENT

The European settlement of what eventually became the United States was, to say the least, a furiously energetic process. Much of the continent was politically swallowed up by a national entity based in Washington, D.C., an entity whose gigantic steps across the continent, from Virginia to Louisiana and westward to the Pacific Ocean, have been made into the subject of many books, films, and television shows. But furious, onrushing settlement of this kind always carried the threat of chaos. What if a whole state decided to secede and join Canada or Mexico? What if the settlers in Utah were Mormons who believed in polygamy? What if certain states became the favorite haunts of racists or neo-Nazis? Such fears of political and social entropy have created, in opposition to the dynamics of settlement, the opposite values of conscious control. Somewhere up in the political tree — which we believe is probably located anywhere except in the city of Washington — sit the wise men and women who help see to it that Americans are inclined to support rather than erode or destroy their political institutions.

Even today, much of American political debate is dominated by these opposite values of expansion and control. Americans worry nonstop about getting even bigger and better. Then, as quantitative expansion reaches its apogee, they are seized with the fear that their expansion may have a destructive edge. All those mighty factories are polluting heaven and earth! The oceans themselves are becoming saturated with our garbage! The president, Americans sometimes proclaim, should appoint a wise person, a czar devoted to curbing our bad industrial and agricultural habits — the inevitable fruits of trying to earn more by making more!

As the above suggests, America is a land that can easily be parodied. That is why so many entertainers spend so much of their time doing just that. But the American "experiment" is so powerful precisely because it allows its citizens to make fun of it. Such an ability strongly suggests an underlying note of confidence that somehow goes beyond all the conflicts — between races, between religions, between occupations, and between those living in cities, suburbs, and farmland. That note of confidence is based, I believe, more on certain abstract ideals — even the ideals of the Declaration of Independence and the Constitution.

Americans share something very important: a powerful allegiance to the pragmatic ideals called fairness and justice. That is why they instinctively turn to eliminate injustice of any kind from their society. As even American critics like to point out, such faith in the judiciary is very unwise. It idealizes governmental figures — judges — with very human limitations. But Americans see their judiciary in evangelistic rather than merely political terms, as a force aglow with religious feeling (much as this feeling is denied in everyday life). The

judge in his black robe, clutching a heavy wooden gavel, is not just a "judge" — he is an almost allegorical embodiment of the spirit of justice. But for these wise and impartial judges, runs the American myth, Americans would all be shooting each other in the streets.

REMAKING REALITIES

One generalization only remains to be stated: Insofar as America is an experiment, it also is a discussion of the nature of reality. The American lust for triumph is nowhere as obviously displayed as in the American passion for remaking "superficial realities." In Las Vegas, for example, the architecture of New York plays a major role in decorating the brightly lit streets. In the New York borough of Manhattan, restaurants vie to look and to feel like those of Paris or Provence. By using the Internet, Americans can experience types of religious meditation and ecstasy that would otherwise eat up thousands of dollars' worth of airplane tickets. Anything can be simulated, recreated, or transmogrified, the American spirit seems to declare. There are no limits to how we can modify the environment we are used to.

As we all know, this supreme American adaptability, which obviously overlaps with Americans' enthusiasm for the media, has often been criticized — especially by those Europeans fired up with cultural ideals that trace back to such 19th-century writers as Thomas Carlyle, John Ruskin, and Matthew Arnold. The European cultural ideal is humanistic — which easily can be translated as antimechanical. Mechanism, meanwhile, is the secret engine of America's limitless adaptability. But, as we might expect — since so much of what we have been saying is about defenses as well as direct expressions — Americans are the ones who developed academic programs in the humanities in ways that affect every American undergraduate.

In a deeper and more carefully thought-through sense, is it possible to speak of a genuine American humanism? Can one see at work in America's technological triumphs a force of character that still pays homage to the individual human soul, with all of its eccentricities and

irregularities? In other words, does the Bill of Rights represent a real or merely a superficial organization of human experience?

The answer to these questions is not an easy one. Americans so often criticize their own failings as a nation driven by public relations, entertainment, and mere *seeming* as opposed to *being.* But the capacity to criticize in this way — to question the apparent basics of one's culture — implies a humanistic quality, and perhaps the most important one of all. Every American tends to respond with pride when he contemplates the nation's Founding Fathers, who took on the king of England and handed his armies a humiliating defeat. Americans who feel this way include those who declare that they are politically radical as well as those who characterize themselves as ultraconservatives.

What Americans most deeply share, in short, is the honor they pay to the individual — the single person deciding for himself what values to espouse, what faith to follow. This qualifies, I believe, as a form of humanism. It also has its dangers — as is shown each time a young American person with a gun begins to fire the weapon in a public school. But the risk is commensurate with the benefit. Uphold the supreme importance of the single individual citizen, and you can look forward to a life of creative disturbance!

The Great Tradition
is a Great Bag of Tricks

As THE PRESIDENT of a large university, I spend most of my time with small problems. A department feels ill treated and, by the time the negotiations and soothing are over, I have spent so much time thinking about a specific mission or curriculum or petty-cash budget of that department that all the other departments have effectively vanished. The same is true of the many other burning issues I face — like whether three additional security cameras are worth more or less than one resurfaced basketball court.

It boils down to a problem of focus. You can't see all of America when you're in the depths of Death Valley or at the heights of Mount Rainier. Thus, when I try to focus on the future of higher education in America, I experience a panicky vertigo and a desire to say something like, "Can't we solve this problem by enlarging some part of our budget?"

Your invitation to offer some thoughts about a vessel as large as the ship of American higher education as it sails into the future, therefore, was a godsend. In other words, it got me thinking. I thought that we really have to begin to get ready for something new.

Speech to the Millennium Conference at the College of Staten Island, February 15, 2000

Let me give you a perspective on what I mean by looking at how academic life used to be. My example is from my undergraduate days at Columbia, just across the harbor and up the river from here.

Columbia, in my day, was famous for its undergraduate program in the humanities. It was also known as teaching the Great Tradition and it was daunting. We were, for example, given just one weekend to read the *Iliad* in Richmond Lattimore's English translation. Though most of us had become speed readers in high school, we found this talent did little to prepare us for an assignment like this. As Sunday night began to approach Monday morning, with most of us still stuck somewhere in Book 16, it became grimly obvious we were not going to reach the end of Book 24 in time.

Somehow, we learned anyway. But closer inspection taught us something else. The humanities were in fact the *western humanities* — from Homer to Plato to Saint Augustine to Dante to Shakespeare to Tolstoy. The faculty teaching Asian literature and history were lobbying either to get their texts into the humanities program or to have a separate Oriental humanities program.

At the time, I thought it was a good idea. Why not add the *Bhagavad-Gita* and *Rashoman* and Persian architecture and Chinese military history to keep company with the Bible and *Hamlet* and Chartres Cathedral and the Duke of Wellington? I changed my mind at the time because I thought the inevitable result would be a curriculum so overstuffed it would slide into chaos and shallowness. Sticking with the western humanities, therefore, was a defensive step that also coincided with the western value we know as *coherence*.

I look back on those days with nostalgia because our world is taking a new direction. Part of the coherence of my education was that it took place right on campus, through books and slides and lectures. Academic travel was important to scholars — to professors and perhaps even Ph.D. candidates — but not expected of students. Original pictures and texts were often to hard to get to or get a hold of once even in the same town. A graduate student guide, said to have been written by Jacques Barzun, whose intellectual prowess ran

neck and neck with God's, warned sardonically that a clever graduate student would not choose a topic requiring research in the archives of the Kremlin. Uptown Manhattan would do just fine.

How the world has changed! Today the archives of the Kremlin lie open. And today we can read Stalin's hand-written notes on the latest purges of Trotskyites. We owe the former of these changes to the demise of the Soviet Union. We owe the latter to what we now call the virtual world. Those notes in Stalin's hand — if they really exist — can no doubt be called up on a computer screen at home. At home, not in the Kremlin, and not even on the Columbia campus! Imagine that. Well, we can imagine that and just about anything else. We are becoming titans or demigods of knowledge. All the information you may ever need and all the expertise to guide you is right there on your screen.

As evidence of what I am saying, I offer a story from a recent edition of *The New York Times* called "Suddenly, Everybody's An Expert."

> Oscar Wilde is said to have defined an expert as an ordinary man away from home giving advice. Today, those words may be truer than ever, with a few tweaks. An expert, it seems, is now an ordinary person sitting at home, beaming advice over the Internet to anyone who wants help ... They are participating in a new breed of Web site that tries to match people who have questions with people who think they have answers.

The *Times* could have added that post-secondary education is in the process of taking a dramatic leap. The entire planet is in the process of turning itself into an educational institution, the faculty of which consists of the entire human species. More and more members of the species are in continual, and sometimes continuous, touch with one another in a virtual schoolhouse.

This suggests the word "virtual" has a synonym or at least incorporates another word. That word is "universal." Like it or not, the fact you have found something that was buried in a library or a monastery

or a government archive on the other side of the earth is no longer merely meritorious. What is meritorious is transmitting your find all around the world. *That* is scholarship. At least that is scholarship to people, in the words of the *Times* article, "who *think* they have answers" and who may have no academic training or scholarly credentials.

No wonder our universities are having a hard time of it. To keep up with the information revolution, they are actually having to become universal in the struggle to keep up with their students. This new state of affairs can be easily dismissed as just a matter of technique. Trudging up and down the stacks of the library is really no different from trudging, in your pajamas, from your bed to the computer.

Not really. The Internet refreshes itself more often than the library acquires new books. Sources are known in traditional academia, but not always on the Internet. The change of technique is keeping company with a change of content and a change of authority. At the same time, an expansion of knowledge, especially in the sciences, is cutting a lot of old mooring lines that held the ship of American education fast.

DNA research may contribute to a transformation of our notions of how the world's peoples actually are related to each other and give us understandings about migrations and languages. Archaeology suggests that the visitors from Scandinavia and Spain were not the first persons from elsewhere to set foot in the Americas. Nor, it seems, were the people who crossed the land-bridge from what we now call Siberia to what we now call Alaska. They may have all been beaten to the punch by boat people who somehow crossed the Pacific.

Speaking of crossing oceans, we no longer doubt the validity of the theory of plate tectonics — the idea that the earth's surface is actually made of large masses that have moved apart, creating separate oceans, and collided — and that, for example, the collision of India with the mainland of Asia created the Himalayas. And that these movements continue to create earthquakes and to reshape the world.

We now also ask what might lie *beyond* the universe. Not long ago, we thought the universe endless, limitless, infinite. Now we know it is curved and may have an end and someday an astronaut will break through the wall and either be hailed by the Heavenly Choir as the new Lindbergh or told sternly to go home and keep his nasty Planet Earth problems to himself.

We can call this globalism or, better still, universalism or even a non-prejudicial approach to the truth. But as a shift of perspective, this new and embracing view of life is what we, the nation's academics, are going to have to cope with from now on.

The problem boils down to this: How do you get the *universe*, of all things, into a college classroom? Let me offer a couple of answers.

First, abolish the classroom. The kids are hooked up to the Internet anyway, aren't they? They can do their work at home, or wherever.

Second, admit that we live in a visual rather than a literary age. So, let's use pictures, on room-sized screens if need be, to immerse our students so deeply in other cultures of the human past and present that they will cry out with wonder and joy, "It's better than MTV." Correction: "It's *cooler* than MTV!"

And third, let's redesign our courses so they have the feel and aura of quiz shows. Why not? "Who Wants to be a Millionaire?" draws gazillions of viewers, fascinated, involved, avid. TV is interesting and fun already. So let's make it educational as well. Because right now, higher education is playing Al Gore to TV's Fred Astaire.

Well, maybe not. It's too vulgar, isn't it? Can my zippy version of education really work? Can you learn about ancient Greece just by looking at images of temples, vases, coins, and even an occasional manuscript? Well, yes, in part, you might say, because we already show slides and pictures, but that's still only part of it. But then I ask, does such a purely visual education match up with reading the *Oresteia* of Aeschylus? No, you say. And I agree. But, that visual experience might serve as a wonderful prelude to reading Aeschylus and a worthy companion to his plays.

In other words, the gauntlet has been thrown down before us. We have to pick it up, buckle on our armor, and ride into battle. But *not* into battle with the idea of entertainment or the idea that education can be entertaining. We don't have to — because we have in our saddlebags the most *entertaining* bag of tricks ever invented. It's *still* known as the Great Tradition, including now both the western and eastern traditions. What these traditions tell us about the human mind and the human heart is fascinating, complex, and always new.

What we have to battle with is ourselves, with our expectations that what we have done heretofore we will do henceforward. Rather turgid prose, no? Let's avoid it and let's equally avoid turgid instruction. And it's so easy to avoid that and to make learning exciting. Our great documents and works of art include fathers on the verge of killing their sons, kings so lustful they send their rivals to sure death in battle, men who make the mistake of sleeping with their mothers, and endless characters whose idea of fun is mayhem, rape, torture, conquest, and murder. Give your 18-year-old students stories like these — otherwise known as the stories of Abraham, David, and Oedipus, to name the obvious ones — and watch them drool and ask for more.

I am proposing to you today what I believe is an overdue revision of the scholastic approach. A visual generation is languishing, and not doing all that well, with a great deal of literary material. Why not use the virtual world's advantages, especially in imagery, to promote the still indisputable advantages of the literary? Why not reorient the academic compass so its needle always points in the direction of sheer delight? Let us tell our students that learning and knowledge are entertaining and delightful. If you've ever watched a baby learn something simple, you've seen that delighted glory. That glory, and the desire for it, do not leave us with age.

Let us tell our students that when they get through experiencing our virtually reconstructed ancient Greek plays performed in virtually reconstructed ancient Greek theatres, they will have the chance — if they're good enough — to take ancient Greek language on the Internet and to amaze us when they quote the words of Achilles in

the original. We picked up the gauntlet. Let's throw it down at their feet. I think they will pick it up.

But I suspect a question is nibbling at our ankles: Can we fit all that much *thinking* into an undergraduate curriculum? Well, maybe we need to redefine what we want our undergraduates to accomplish. Traditionally, we have expected them to pass their courses. An exceptional few got big pats on the back for actually doing an original piece of work as an undergraduate.

That outlook may have been acceptable in the bad old days, but in the good new days ahead we should begin considering the notion that any high school student who hopes to get into our university must have made, by the time he or she graduates from high school, at least one original and personal discovery. We could call it the Pre-collegiate Thesis. Of course, it could take the form of a painting or a symphony or a drama on video. It could take any form, provided it showed thought leading to discovery. One thing is sure: Our admissions officers will want to experience those theses a lot more than they want to experience SAT scores, 10-page lists of extracurricular activities, and how the applicant did in sophomore Spanish.

This is not very far removed from the way things are now. The students we are admitting already know a lot about thinking and criticizing and drawing distinctions. They can't watch TV or listen to the radio or get into a chat room without hearing debate and interviews and polemic. An atmosphere of non-stop analysis and skepticism such as we now take for granted is going to stamp on our young citizens of the United States such an intellectual curiosity as American higher education has never had to deal with before. You may despair of your students sometimes because they seem to know nothing, have read nothing. But watch them leave your classroom and head for a computer to prove what you just said is wrong, wrong, w-r-o-n-g. That is curiosity and, of course, a youthful desire to beat age.

Good, use it. Curiosity and even, in many cases, critical, analytic thinking has sneaked up on us when we weren't looking and quietly occupied our nation and our society. Thinking is everywhere! More to the point, being and sounding thoughtful is good, not a sign that you are getting above yourself. You can walk down the street and hear two ordinary people discussing an election, with one saying, "His positions are inconsistent," and the other responding, "I think he's trying to corral the feminist vote without losing the right-wing gorillas." Insights once reserved for seminars and high-class dinner parties are all over the place.

A part of me does not like what I have just said. There are still plenty of crude monstrosities of popular culture avidly lapped up by millions and millions of our fellow citizens. But then I remember something else. I remember the position of *The New York Times* when I was growing up in Brooklyn.

People who read the *Daily News*, the *New York Post*, the *Journal-American*, and the *World Telegram and Sun* had one thing in common. They did not read the *Times*. That was for the rich and clever people who lived and worked "downtown." I mean, the *Times* had few pictures and no comics and didn't have special columns for teachers and transit workers. If you could get through the *Herald Tribune*, why that made you a hero or even an intellectual of sorts.

Today, the *Times* is a regional paper, and giving *The Washington Post* a run for its money in the District of Columbia. It has become the bearer of a *lingua franca*, the language (and paper) you of course read if you are even half serious about your life and career.

That's some evidence of what I mean when I say we have become a thinking society, a college society, even possibly an intellectual society. It follows from our history of being a democratic — with a small "d" — society and from the recent history of colleges and universities opening their doors to those other than the privileged.

Turning higher education into a mass phenomenon coincided with the great economic expansion of America after the war. That's something we all have digested as recent history. It did something else few of us noticed until recently. It blanketed the country with a dense net of colleges and universities, informally but efficiently integrated, that were thriving on people who wanted to learn how to

think and to think intelligently. Moreover, it was the beginning of a cumulative process.

Many of the students who arrived on campus after the war were the first in their families to do so. They strategized with their children to get into even better colleges. As for the third generation of college-goers, they are the students we are trying so hard to attract now — and their internal maps have big crosses on a locale called graduate school or law school or business school. They are serious and they are thoughtful.

What we need to do, I think, is clear. The Great Tradition is not a piece of marble, though it includes some wonderful marble statues. Nor is it static, remote, and over. It continues. It lives. It can be, as I hope I have persuaded you, entertaining. And it can live in harmony with our new virtual world. It is our job — no, it is our *duty* to combine the wizardry of the information age with the magic inside the Great Tradition's bag of tricks for the next wave of our thinking society.

The New Entrepreneurial
University

THIS IS DAUNTING. Here is a roomful of experienced university administrators, so devoted to their profession that they join the AAUA and encourage one another to behave sensibly. And facing this roomful of experience and good sense I find ... myself, a university president whose administrative history appears to be a collection of stories and personal idiosyncrasies. What, I have been worrying, can I possibly say that you do not already know?

I have walked the floor and talked to myself in hopes of finding a topic. And, like any hard-working obsessive-compulsive, I have come up with five. But I can place all of them under an umbrella I will call *the new entrepreneurial university*. Here they are.

Number One: *The new entrepreneurial university is turning out to be a place that makes money.*

Think back only 50 years, as those of us over 60 are learning to do, and you will encounter a world of higher education in which the concept of money was controversial or at least impolite. True, one

Opening remarks to the American Association of University Administrators at its Assembly XXVII held in Philadelphia, June 24-27, 1999

expected something called a *paycheck* at appropriate intervals. But the idea that it was compensation for some vulgar artifact called *services rendered* was nearly unthinkable. In that world, the connection between work and pay had been rendered mysterious or taboo.

That sundering also distorted the obvious — that faculty and administrators were really engaged in the same enterprise. Rather than seeing one another as different components of the same organism, they looked upon one another as members of a different species. Thus, faculties were forever opposed to the sinister machinations of administrators, who did little more, faculty critics believed, than produce ill-conceived memoranda, in sextuplicate, which required a response in same. Meanwhile, a sneering administrator could observe that Murchison of economics was caught groping a sophomore — the president's niece, no less! — and his publications list would now include abundant press clippings.

The reason faculty and administration were tangling was that neither group quite understood the fragility of the boat in which they were both sailing. The GI Bill and the war-time contracts that had been converted to grants sent torrents of money into their pockets, giving them fairy-tale wealth. They main problem they faced, or so they thought, was how to deal with the even greater torrent of students who came pouring onto campuses in record numbers from 1950 to about 1970 — and what to teach them.

It was a legitimate concern, but only one. The other was the fairy-tale money, because that's what it was, yet they believed it would always be there. Was it, then, any great wonder universities started feeling like the Titanic, impervious to any danger, fore or aft? Probably not. But their little boat ran into its own iceberg, and I needn't rehearse for you all the financial problems we faced from 1970 to about 1990. But one good thing emerged from those 20 or so vexing years. Vivid experience taught faculty and administrators that if one of them kicked a hole in the bottom of the boat, they'd both go down with the ship.

You and I, as members of the American Association of University Administrators, are the beneficiary generation of that long-coming accommodation. We take for granted, by and large, a level of cooperation among all of those on the university payroll that would once have been dismissed as mad fantasy. We are the luckiest university administrators in living memory, I guess.

The high level of internal cooperation we take for granted — after all due allowance for the ridiculous vendettas and feuds that continue to occupy some faculty club lunch tables — in turn helps us to understand why universities today can pull in a lot of money. A rich donor, wanting to endow a special library collection, will be more impressed with your university if the well-turned-out vice president for development is accompanied by a scholar who knows what the library actually means. The scientist seeking a grant will have better chances of winning it if the administration has provided, and maintained, the research infrastructure the proposed work will require. This kind of cooperation applies to public as well as private institutions, because the former are giving the latter a real run for their money these days in matters of private donations.

At the same time, most professors and administrators, especially those nearing the age of retirement, have as much incentive as any other person for becoming closely acquainted with the workings of the American economy and the likelihood of financial survival in retirement. Both sides have come to understand the connection between income and expense. This, in turn, allows communication on money matters between faculty and administrators to take place under the auspices of reason rather than of emotion.

Now you may hear that a public university should not be grubbing for money. Their work is teaching not fund raising, you'll hear. Tell that to the state legislature! And only let the university's football team start moving up in the rankings, and the skeptics won't even ask why rich people are buying up all the houses around the university and its stadium ... and giving more generously to the alumni fund. And that brings me to topic ...

Number Two: *The new entrepreneurial university is a place where you can legally talk about your students as "customers."*

Having passed the age of 60, I can actually remember when you got a strange look if you referred to a student, of all people, as a *customer*. You were a customer when you went to Katz's Deli for a pastrami on rye. You were even a customer when you purchased an intangible, like life insurance. But the academy, which drapes you in the fashions of the middle ages on commencement day, did not see you as something so mundane, even though you had purchased, at high cost, an intangible. You were a bachelor, a master, or a doctor. But you were not a customer.

Today, we are more likely to say of students, "What else could they be?" They pay us tuitions for an education we promise them and describe in detail in our publications. And if they decide they don't like what we are selling, they can hand it right back to us and buy their education, like their pastrami, elsewhere.

Samuel Johnson said, "When a man knows he is to be hanged in a fortnight, it concentrates his mind wonderfully." Our equivalent hanging — dealing with students and their families as customers — has concentrated the thinking of America's universities no less wonderfully. Those on their payrolls — faculty, administrators, staff — could now actually make the connection between the money in their paychecks and the kids cluttering up the campus.

Those at the more junior end of university administration should savor what this new state of affairs has meant for them. Not very long ago, a bright idea coming from a young administrator, neatly diagrammed in a chart, was quite likely to go unread by that young person's superiors. It had nothing going for it, but the fact that it would save some money or earn a quick million. It was nowhere near so interesting as the text of the dean's remarks being prepared for the annual Christmas tea.

In today's money-obsessed world, where university presidents hear the word *money* from the moment they open their eyes in the morning to the moment, often 18 hours later, when they close them for the night, such a suggestion would rise quickly through the chain

of command. And were it to prove workable, the response from on high would consist of thanks, congratulations, and possibly — on some occasions, anyway — a pay raise.

I admit that a school run by Moses or Socrates or St. Thomas More would be altogether different. It would cost less, and tuition could be paid in garlic, apples, or oxen. But it would be open to the few and teach few subjects, however worthy they might be. Our society demands many educated people, not just a literate and philosophical elite, and needs to command a great range of knowledge and wisdom. Consequently, we have to think about income and expenditure almost as much as did the people who built the great cathedrals of the middle ages. Thinking about money — and chasing it — has made our universities the wonders they are. And something else: When we talk openly about money it loses its mystery. Which leads me to topic ...

Number Three: *In the new entrepreneurial university, faculty and administrators increasingly resemble each other and have often been in college or graduate school together.*

There was a generation of university administrators we can barely remember today. They began their careers in the 1920s and 1930s when conditions weren't exactly encouraging, and lived to see the invasion within the halls of ivy of the ex-GIs and then emerging ethnics — Poles and Italians, imagine, with Ph.D.s! These were students and young faculty who could scarcely understand the concept of a fine tweed jacket or the glories of a spring day in Paris. Yet they were staring at old-style disciplinarians, whose jackets had been handed down from their grandfathers, and they weren't blinking.

Today's administrators grew out of that invasion or are the children of those invaders. Having similar degrees from similar schools and having undergone similar experiences to get where they are, they do not regard faculty as a different species. More to the point, the remnant of faculty that persists in the archaic notion that administrators know nothing of scholarship is finding its case harder to make and finding, as well, a smaller audience for it.

And that is why I think we should all savor this moment in academic administration. We benefit daily from what I call the "double-barreled" effect of academic entrepreneurship. You do a good job because you hold yourself up to your personal standards, which are very high. Then, having taken joy and pride in living up to yourself and your reputation, you discover you've had a real effect on the bottom line. And that effect is not abstract, not at all. It may mean, for example, that three adjuncts who were going to lose their jobs can be retained. It means the university can finally re-seed the south lawn, otherwise know as "the big muddy."

I hope that someday, and soon, the effectiveness of faculty and administration *as a team* will supplant from the *Wall Street Journal* and *The Harvard Business Review* articles about political correctness on the campus next door where one professor is actually teaching feminist readings of the Koran. The teamwork of professors and administrators, not only in fund raising but also in the general operation of the university, is the story. And I think it is a big one. Which leads me to topic ...

Number Four: *In the new entrepreneurial university, we have finally succeeded in making living contact with the world we purport to be teaching our students about.*

Half a century ago, and even more recently, it was commonplace for Old Professor Grizzle or Not-So-Old Professor Graytemples to produce from a briefcase yellow, crumbling notes first produced at dear old State at about the time he was just beginning to grow a beard. They would recite their ancient thoughts as if they were a bard reciting Homer. Except Homer has the contrary tendency of waking you up and exciting you.

The students, amazingly, weren't rebelling. That came later. Maybe they didn't want to hurt the old boy's feelings. But that should not keep us from celebrating the fact that such a scene is almost inconceivable in the new entrepreneurial university. It is so for several reasons. We ask our students to evaluate our teachers. We ask the teachers to work hard on their communication skills. We update and advance our curricula to keep instruction fresh and to

keep up with customer demand. And are we ever lucky! A thought that leads me to topic ...

Number Five: *In the new entrepreneurial university, despite complaints about the decline of our outward status, our status has actually grown greater.*

If we could return to a university around 1950, you would be amazed at how many compliments good teachers and scholars were used to receiving in an average day. Working in a university was a good place to get patted on the back. Sometimes the pat was a promotion. Sometimes it was called tenure. Often it was students thanking you for making the Ottoman Empire come alive or teaching them the beauty — and harmlessness — of calculus. The course you helped get them into saved their lives and you or someone restored their faith in education.

Today's university has given up much of that automatic praise. It's common to hear academics complain about the sheer rudeness they feel from the world around them. It may on occasion be bad manners, but often they are resenting the amount of administrative handling that is typical of modern civilization and, therefore, of the civilized units called universities.

Ah, but which do you want? To hear that your transcript — you got your degree in 1957 — has, alas, fallen prey to the squirrels as is the fate of so many transcripts? Or to hear from the heartless, soulless, automated registrar's office that your old transcripts, which had been scanned and saved in a computer, will be in the mail tomorrow? It only takes a little money and some good practical sense — handling, if you will — to accomplish this "alienation." But of course, it is no such thing. It is a sign of the university's seriousness.

It is serious business we're in. Universities are critically important to American society. So it is serious business to get along with business leaders and with bureaucrats. It is serious business to listen to our customers and hear what they need and want.

Please savor the beauty of what I am describing to you. Our universities, unlike many in Europe and Asia, are not breeding grounds for discontent, let alone violent revolution. Yet there is

nothing totalitarian about American universities today. We are inclined, I think, to look at our diverse and often strong-willed students and professors and wonder how we ever manage to do anything amid all their chaos and clamor. Yet we do — don't we? — by serving and funding that rich and productive and creative chaos and clamor as well as we can. And given that our universities are the finest in the world, I think we are doing just fine.

The New Millennium

A UNIVERSITY PRESIDENT is expected to be an expert on every-thing, which means the university president is an expert on nothing. Neither of these statements is true of this particular university presi-dent. Anyone who expects me to be an expert on everything having to do with The George Washington University and higher education is either paying me a compliment I do not deserve or setting me up to fail.

The idea that a university president must necessarily be an expert in nothing is equally untrue or misleading. I certainly don't pretend to possess up-to-date expertise in economics or physics or biology or law, even though I have a law degree. But — like my brother and sister university presidents — I do claim an expert knowledge *about* what is going on at my university. It's an expertise in perspective, and a basic qualification for the job.

Using this perspective carries over to looking at, and trying to understand, something about the American national character. Our universities, after all, reflect our nation: They are very different from European or Asian universities, just as our culture is different from Europe's and Asia's. We are more inclined to risk chaos than to submit to regimentation.

Speech to the Skidmore Daylight Lodge # 237 (Masons), February 6, 2001

This character trait of individuality is in the American grain. We owe it to the Founding Generation — the generation of Jefferson, Madison, Adams, Jay, Franklin, Mason, and Washington. The Declaration of Independence first stated the basic principle, then the Constitution made it formal and legal: We have rights as individuals.

For more than two centuries, the idea of rights has only expanded. The expansion of rights, especially in the 20th century, had the habit on occasion of turning dangerous, of becoming anarchy, terrorism, chaos, or civil war. "I know my rights" became a war cry that anyone could use. The problem, of course, is that aggressive assertions of ego and personality always wind up bumping into other people's assertions of exactly the same qualities. In other words, your rights don't come at the expense of my rights.

Those of us in academia, who've been around for a few years, remember with a shudder the scenes we had to deal with in the 1960s and '70s — the sit-ins, the protests, the general carryings-on that turned campuses into battlefields. All that subsided, but left permanent changes in the national and the academic landscapes and characters. In one of those "pendulum of history" movements that high school teachers used to love to point out for us, what seemed to fill the place left by student radicalism was a middle-aged neo-conservatism.

This movement tried to emphasize a classic American tradition, certainly traceable to the Founders, that every citizen bore as a birthright a great burden of personal responsibility. Since the Constitution protected against tyranny, individuals had the responsibility of governing themselves, of resisting appeals to rebellion and anarchy, and of using their freedom as the agent of their good impulses, not their bad ones.

Although they were known as neo-conservatives, the great preachers of this movement were classic liberals in the sense that Adam Smith, Thomas Jefferson, and John Stuart Mill were liberals. These great historic figures gave us what we call to this day "liberal democracy," forms of government where the rights of the individual are paramount. But the great liberal tradition ran into perhaps its greatest challenge as

the 20th century was ending. The challenge consisted of a global electronic universe that was often described equally by those who loved it and those who hated it as a force that enormously expanded the power of the individual. It also proved a benefit to institutions, including governments, corporations, and universities.

The Internet had a keen effect on universities. On the one hand, the Internet helped in all kinds of mundane ways, from extending teaching and research activities to registering for courses, reading the library catalogue, and finding out what was on the menu in the cafeteria. On the other hand, we worried about our students using the Internet to do harm to computer networks or individuals. Around the world, we knew that acts of mischief and terror could be planned and perhaps carried out over the Internet, so why not on our own campuses?

In other words, we have a very mixed blessing on our hands — and one that is here to stay. And that is where we are right now, tugged one way by our national ideals and character and tugged just as hard by the technology that does not by nature have either ideas or character. Let me tell you what I mean by that. The Internet, for all we say about it, is a medium, a means of communication, a technique for moving something from here to there. In that sense, it is no different from a telephone or a television — or a sewer pipe. All of them, from the Internet to the pipe, carry what we put into them. They come with no content of their own, no point of view of their own, no ideals, and no character of their own. They are neutral.

But we wonder: What if our technology *encourages* others to limit *our* rights and freedoms?[1] We value the rights that allow us to explore the world as we will, in the privacy of our homes, offices, campus residences. But what if the process of exploration leads some people to anti-social or terrorist actions?

What can we do, and what must we do, to prepare our children and our young people for a world in which some of them can do a lot of damage to our society — to its resources and psyche — at a young age?

[1] Editing this speech eight months after I gave it and just shortly after September 11, 2001, this question seems more poignant than ever.

As a university president, I routinely encourage ethics courses with titles like "Ethics in Our Technological Age." This is the kind of expertise that, I believe, a university president must have. He may not be in a position to teach such a course, but he must know *about* it and have an expert sense of its applicable value. Such courses endeavor to teach students that if they succeed in disabling computers used by others, they themselves may not be very happy with the results. It is really a restatement in technological terms of the teachings of Rabbi Hillel and Jesus, which have been distilled for us as the Golden Rule.

I support courses like this, however, because they do not expect students to accept a prescription as a matter of religious faith. To the contrary, they discuss the world in which we actually live today and the way technology is transforming it — and then, critically, the place of the individual in both the transformation and the transformed society. It requires individuals — students, in this case — to see that individuals are part of something larger, something we may call society or the world or just the campus. And I will add, by the way, that courses like this renew my belief that computer technologies and distance learning will never replace the value of face-to-face education. Meeting in classrooms draws individuals out of their isolation, requires them to confront other ideas and to defend their own. Perhaps it even contributes to being a sane member of society.

I should add, also, that supporting courses on contemporary ethics in college does *not* justify a failure to teach ethical concepts to children from the age of five. Parents who give their children access to the Internet — and it seems to start right out of the cradle — know to warn them about risks and dangers, including breaking the law. Do not steal someone's information, they learn, don't damage anything or anyone. But that is not ethics. That is good citizenship or self-protection, like minding traffic lights and flossing.

But in a world that is transforming, good citizenship and self-protection, though worthy, are by themselves inadequate. There may be, in the electronic transformation of human societies, some ideas about ethical teaching and ethical connections. Let me lay this out for a minute or two.

We have all grown accustomed to calling up a business and having someone on the other end of the phone call up our account on a screen in a matter of seconds. We watch a football game and learn how many people have so far walked through the gates, even though we've yet to see the kickoff. We read the morning paper or turn on the morning TV shows, and we are not surprised — in fact, we expect — to have news form China or Australia ... because we know that news might affect how much money our stock portfolios are worth today or the likelihood of our traveling to one of those places next week.

We are wired up — locally and globally — because we really are connected. The trick now, it seems to me, is to convert this approach, which often seems fear-laden and nervous, into a new and more positive spirit that will enable a new kind of ethical training for the young and for the rest of us.

Imagine, for example, that our elementary schools created electronic circles that would include a few dozen children of the same age from all around the world. Imagine a kind of mini-world that parallels the larger world all of us read about daily in the papers.

Inject, then, into these circles an ethical component, perhaps in the form of instant messaging or chat rooms for the children who belong to the circles. Let them propose questions about behavior and answer them. Right now, we insist our schools do more than teach language and numbers to our children. We insist they "socialize" them as well — and well they should. And why should the schools not also become the means for global socialization of the young, for exposing them to unbounded and international senses of abiding by the law and behaving ethically?

An idea. One of many to come, I hope.

And I can imagine, without trying very hard, some of the negative reactions such an idea would arouse in some American hearts, and others, too. Aren't you trying, they might say, to slip international government in the back door? Won't you make American children more loyal to their foreign friends than to their sovereign government?

Objections like those tend to see anything *international* as a response to something bad. Thus, we have international cooperation to fight crime and the drug trade and the true villains like Slobodan Milosevic. We may even take international action to fight global warming or AIDS. But in a broad sense, this is more like police action than mutuality, than the Golden Rule. We want to hunt down and destroy the drug lords. We want to hunt down and destroy AIDS. And so we should.

But we should no less understand that mutual cooperation is not always a police action. We have opportunities that have to do with sharing, mutual dialogue, and a deeper understanding of legitimate differences. In other words, can all of these frightening terms — internationalism, globalization, cyberspace — affect us in positive ways?

We know already they can, but we incline to the negative. I think this new century must be the time when the questions I have just raised — and others — will cease to be debating points and become instead points of departure for policy making, including how we raise our children and how we go about instilling an ethical sense in them that will guide them in the world as it is.

This is serious business in light of the great paradox of our age. Never before have so many human beings been alive on the planet. And never before have so many individuals, or small groups, had so much power at their fingertips, in large part because of a computer. To put it differently, on the one hand, earth from afar must look like a beehive swarming with activity. But we know bees and ants and termites all share in a consciousness of the whole — together they make up an organism.

We are not quite like that. All our swarming around the hive we call earth is not aimed at one goal. We are a species of a different kind, a more individual kind, and becoming even more so as technology and knowledge transform us.

What we need to learn now is how to transform our ethical systems so they serve us as the beings we are and are becoming. To serve us as we really are.

    I know the questions I have raised and the imperatives I have stated have a heroic ring to them. But I address you as brother Masons and remind you that if we weren't inclined to heroism, we would not have become Masons. Our heroism has to begin here — with ourselves, with our children, with our grandchildren — because from here and with them perhaps we can transform the world.

Managing

in

Higher

Education

Great Expectations: Expanding Demands on the Campus Leader

NOW, MORE THAN at any other time in history, America's colleges and universities are in hot demand. Despite the recent downturn in the stock market, the safe bet is still on a college degree, preferably an advanced degree, as a prerequisite to success. Given that, we can further assert that the *intramural* decisions made by college and university administrators are of great *extramural* concern. That, in turn, has opened the door to expanded expectations that campus leaders face in the 21st century.

We have evolved into a "college-educated America." That doesn't mean that the entire population has graduated from a four-year college, but it does mean that enough people have attended a college of some kind that the academic culture is now familiar to every American citizen.

In today's United States, even small-town newspapers take close and careful note of changes in academic admission policies, including the reduction in the emphasis on the SAT. They report on the opening

Reprinted with permission from *The Presidency*, Fall 2001

of a new community college in almost the same breathless tone they would use if the college were a multiplex cinema. Meanwhile, a local student who gains admission to Columbia or George Washington or UCLA is likely to be the subject of an in-depth feature.

As a college-educated society, the country demands more reporting, and smarter reporting, about academic matters. The result has been that today's senior academic administrator is almost morbidly aware of media coverage. Fifty years ago, most campuses made the news only at commencement time, and then mainly because of the famous people scheduled to deliver speeches. Today, the academic leaders can be forgiven their feelings that the media are vultures, perched in the trees around the campus, waiting for something terrible to happen. The campus quad is a "story waiting to happen," particularly if that story entails student tragedy.

For college and university administrators, the good news is that they finally live in a country that pays attention to them. The bad news is — as it has always been — that attention can take many different forms. A sophisticated, college-aware public still takes Athenian pleasure in seeing the high and mighty brought down.

As these changes have taken place, campus leaders, from presidents on down, have watched their roles become steadily more demanding. In the middle of the 20th century, college and university presidents were still somewhat ceremonial figures, best known for their eloquent rhetoric at commencement. Then a novel rumor started to make the rounds: More and more academic presidents were serving as fund raisers, as public relations troubleshooters, and as major expressions of the "institutional image."

Slowly but surely a transition has taken place. An expanded college and university system, drawing more public scrutiny and serving an expanded national economic system, requires an expanded presidential role. Faculty members occasionally protest that today's president has too much power and influence. At the same time, it has become increasingly difficult to imagine an academic system that does not have its president on duty 24 hours a day, seven days a week.

You can call this a redefinition of the presidential function. What it amounts to is that the president has to deal, on shorter and shorter notice, with all kinds of offices located in such parts of the extracurricular society as business, government, and the courts. In fact, the entire academic establishment is integrating itself ever more broadly and effectively with the world's most productive and powerful society.

EVOLVING THE METAPHOR

If we had to name the most important academic developments of the 20th century, we could do a lot worse than to suggest that they centered on the steady integration of America's colleges and universities with America itself. When the century began, our higher education institutions still had a deeply elitist look to them. They were academies for maintaining and replenishing a tiny group of leaders, leaders who could move smoothly between the Oval Office and the boardrooms of Chicago, London, or Paris.

By the time the 20th century ended, colleges and universities had been entrusted with training the professional world, and with seeing to it that American experts were at least as brilliant as those to be found anywhere else on our planet.

And, the campus culture has gone from one of isolated intellectualism to one of active engagement with the world at large. This shift is nowhere more apparent than in the president's office. When today's president arrives at the office, phone calls, letters, e-mail, and faxes can be expected from almost every corner of the globe. Scandal has to be avoided. Opportunity has to be maximized. The conversations around the table in the president's office often begin to sound like planning sessions for D-Day.

What does all this actually amount to? Can we expect more of the same as higher education institutions find ever newer, fresher, and more abundant ways of connecting with society? Should we, as we define expectations for campus leaders, begin to expect even more qualitative changes?

Finding a plausible answer to these questions requires consideration of prior questions having to do with the nature of knowledge in today's America. Perhaps you've seen predictions that the Internet will abolish the very idea of campus-based higher education. With information being so universal and so available on the Internet — where it is often free of charge — what plausible role remains to be played by campus colleges and universities with live-in presidents and long-term senior administrators?

Another way of articulating this same question is to ask: Are today's higher education students still in need of guidance, or have they turned into the kinds of people who can cope even with the hit-or-miss intellectual environment known as the Internet? To come up with an adequate answer, we must reconsider the college or university image.

Higher education's prevailing metaphor is that of a pipeline, pumping knowledge from those who have it to those who don't. That image has a few advantages. It turns the intellectual aspect of academic life into a convenient mechanism, like its climate-control systems and its various utilities. However, a truer image may also be a less convenient one. The truth is that a campus is in many ways a messy and turbulent place, where challenges to the current consensus are highly regarded, while mere repetitions of traditional ideas are regarded as lacking not only originality but also any power to stimulate.

Our society, as it has turned itself into a college-educated society, has made it far easier for people to think — and sometimes to behave — in a turbulent way. Meanwhile, some people worry about the extent to which ours is becoming a "top-down society" when it comes to communication and the media. A major corporation, we're told, can mobilize public opinion in ways that influence even the president and the Congress of the United States. The 21st century, therefore, may place a new external expectation on campus leaders: to be spokespersons for their constituencies.

A Complex Balance

As the American people have become increasingly college-educated, as they have become increasingly sophisticated about controversy as one of the keys to truth, they stand ready to absorb a new understanding of higher education.

These days, information and the ability to transmit it often look like the obsession of our entire society. Whether the subject is law or medicine, history or literature, anthropology or sociology, those teaching the subject must take repeated account of how opinion on that subject is shaped and transformed through such influences as the media. Yes, every student must acquire the basic intellectual operations, but the student must also learn how to deal with the vast quantities of opinion that he or she is offered by our information-driven world, much of it deserving to be classified as truly brilliant propaganda.

The external expectations for campus leaders must therefore include a complex balance between cooperation and resistance. They must be cooperative and supportive of the "real world" without compromising the values of scholarship — of the ivory tower. Students at every level must learn to work with their society while also learning how to keep their distance from society. Learning for its own sake is vulnerable to the temptations of training for the current marketplace. It can also be dangerous for campus leaders to act like Svengali, exercising who knows what kind of influence on our minds and our values. They must, however, consciously assist society in dealing with what it feels like to be college-educated, which so often means to feel conflicted, which is the same thing as being sophisticated.

Leadership and
Management

WHEN WE DISCUSS leadership and management, when we even use these two words in the same sentence, we come up against an old proposition that these two functions are not at all the same. In fact, they are hostile. A great leader is not the same, possibly the opposite, of the competent bureaucrat known for being a good manager. History, we are told, is full of proof.

A recent historical example gives weight to the proposition. Think of Mikhail Gorbachev, who merely began the evaporation of the Soviet Union in a quiet, systematic, *well-managed* manner. Then think of his replacement, the charismatic Boris Yeltsin, photogenically standing on top of a tank outside the legislature, thundering at the troops inside. That was a leader.

For a while, anyway. Yeltsin's health and neuroses destroyed him finally and left Russia in a state of chaos. That was a leader?

But contrary to the example of Gorbachev and Yeltsin, and contrary to what we may have been told, history is full of proof that

Speech to the U.S. Department of State's 42nd Senior Seminar Assembly on Leadership and Management, April 17, 2000

great leaders also can be good managers. Let me give you three examples, not one of them obscure or, I think, in any way forced.

Alexander the Great reconquered the eastern Mediterranean provinces his father had subdued and which had gone native, beat Darius and the Persian Empire, and bestrode the world of his era as far as the Ganges. As a military leader he was unquestioned and possibly unparalleled. Along the way, he established political and civil management of his empire, centralized enough for him to profit from it, localized enough to permit his appointed governors, or managers, the latitude to make the job worth their while and to guard their Oriental, rather than Hellenic, culture. The military historian General J.F.C. Fuller saw in Alexander's political organization, spanning different countries and cultures, a foreshadowing of the United Nations. Probably an overstatement: sometimes historians fall in love with their subjects.

But it is no overstatement that Alexander understood management. When Alexander died at the age of 33, the *diadochi*, his generals who succeeded him in power, squabbled murderously among themselves, and the empire that Alexander had established so swiftly came apart even more swiftly. They wanted the title of leader without knowing how to manage even themselves.

Another example from history is Charlemagne. He is famous for his military leadership — though one of the greatest works of mediaeval literature concerns the defeat of Roland, the captain of his rearguard, at Ronceval by the Saracens — which first consolidated the Kingdom of the Franks and then thrust outward to form, finally, the Holy Roman Empire. He is still a model of military and political leadership.

But he too was a manager. Illiterate himself, Charlemagne loved learning and brought the monk Alcuin from England to be what we would call more or less his minister of culture. He tried to learn to read, but "could never get the hang of it," yet encouraged literacy in the illiterate knightly class. He also was a great builder of bridges and roads, along the lines of Julius and Augustus Caesar. Marshall McLuhan has referred to Charlemagne's roads as the first mediaeval

"paper routes," making information, the lifeblood of imperial management, possible.

My last example may surprise you. It is Abraham Lincoln. We remember him for prosecuting the Civil War and for his refined and moving language, especially in the Gettysburg Address and the speech at his second inauguration. A model of leadership, we think, in the humblest of packages.

Yet while the war was raging — often not far from where Lincoln tried to sleep at night — he insisted on finishing the Capitol dome. We may take this as a symbolic action and chalk it up to leadership. Fair enough. But it also had the practical value of finishing the house of Congress, getting them to focus on business, because business was not only the war.

It was during the war that Lincoln looked at the plans for the proposed Transcontinental Railroad, approved them, and led Congress to provide the funding — an endlessly complicated piece of business that I will not go into here — to see the railroad built. This was a piece of great management — absorbing the plans, understanding the complexities and difficulties of the project, negotiating with the private builders for the federal subsidies which were justified in opening the country for development and prosperity.

We could add many others as managers and leaders, such as Napoleon and Peter the Great of Russia. We also could, if we choose to, point to great and famous leaders who could manage nothing. And we could point to great managers who needed to be leaders as well, but failed, the saddest example being Herbert Hoover. Thus, history tells us neither one truth nor another, but it does suggest that the greatest or most memorable leaders were good hands at management, too.

How the prejudice that leaders cannot be managers took root is hard to know. A friend suggested it may be a leftover of Romanticism, specifically in its Byronic form of the dark and daring anti-hero who has no patience with the slow and prosaic manager, and next to whom, to be sure, the manager looks dowdy and dull.

Knowing the origin of this prejudice, however, is less important than knowing that it is a prejudice and, like most, it is false.

I think we serve ourselves better if we see that management and leadership *can* be lodged in the same person and, in the best circumstances, they are. Let me at least offer this idea as a hypothesis. And let me undergird the hypothesis with an admission that leadership and management may grow out of inborn qualities, but they have to be developed. Alexander, after all, was the son of a king and his tutor was Aristotle. Those are substantial advantages in development. But there are simpler ways. Take the example of George Washington.

By 1770, Washington had been a vestryman, a justice of the peace, a member of the Virginia House of Burgesses, a delegate to the First and Second Continental Congresses, and of course an experienced soldier and planter, managing a large farm. This recitation I have just given sounds like a résumé, doesn't it? Not as glorious as Alexander's, but solid and very valuable. All throughout Washington's résumé we see opportunities for both leadership and management, sometimes intertwined, and, above all, collegiality.

When we look at history, and especially when we look at daunting historical figures like these, we may be tempted to think that was then and this is now, that the age of heroes is over. Perhaps, but the heart of the matter is that leadership and management combine — can and should combine — in people who are by no stretch of the imagination heroic. In people like you and me.

Promising not to compare myself to Charlemagne or Washington, let me tell you how I think the nexus of leadership and management plays out these days at The George Washington University.

When I came to GW in 1988, I suppose my inner voice was saying, "This place needs vision! Does this place ever need leadership! We've got to shake people up and take some radical measures!" Well, I was right, I think, but another inner voice must have said something, because what I did was not shake people or get renamed Trachtenberg the Terrible. College campuses, like many other institutions, have their

own rhythms. Shaking and radical talk don't lead people — except maybe into their bunkers and foxholes.

So instead, I spent a lot of time running around, shaking hands, and making friends with everyone I could. I helped create new scholarships for students from the District of Columbia. I talked to the media as if GW had been founded slightly *before* Oxford and Cambridge — and the poor dears had never quite caught up.

What I discovered is that leadership, though it certainly requires a vision, has many techniques. The heroic is suited to heroes. Making friends and talking about wonderful possibilities to anyone who will listen is another — and better suited to me. That was a first lesson. And once I had learned it and saw my own approach to leadership had actually started to work, I began to discern the advantages of careful management. I have put these advantages into four compartments though I recognize they are not entirely separate, nor should they be. And anyone may add other compartments.

First, I answer, personally, every letter or memo in my in-box. This is time-consuming and painstaking work, and it would be easy to plead busy-ness. After all, I'm the president of a university, a busy man. So I don't have to respond to a professor when he sends me an article he has just published. But reading it and offering some comments proves to the faculty, not just this professor, that I know who they are, what they are doing, and appreciate them. I conclude that good management of my in-box is the best, perhaps the only, way of retaining my reputation, and authority, as a good leader.

Second, I keep in mind the military truth that great strategy is accomplished only through great tactics. In other words, a change of policy requires careful work on the ground. Officially, a proposal coming from the office of a university president is just a document that must move through certain stages — most critically, faculty approval — before it stands any chance of becoming policy. In practice, however, the actual proposal is the final stage of the campaign that begins with casual references in conversation and careful alignment of trustees, faculty, other administrators, and any incidental actors who may

wander onto the stage. Successful management in this case requires all the leadership qualities of a successful field commander.

I never underestimate the importance of the "incidental image." Books and seminars on management tend to focus on the movement of paper. But you and I are moving, too — in and out of offices, into and out of elevators, up and down the streets. The person in charge is *seen* and is often observed and talked to. What others need to see and talk to is not cardboard or a title with legs and wingtips, but a person and a role model for the entire organization. If you want to turn bureaucrats into dynamic, disciplined managers, then you yourself must project a genuine dynamism and discipline. If you want collegiality, then your conversation must project a genuine energy, good humor, and good judgment. Always remember, never forget: you are not your press clippings. You are what people actually see in the street.

I never stop thinking about the media. It was not very long ago that a university president who showed much interest in his or her school's image was regarded by other university presidents and certainly by faculty as a lout. That was in an age when many reporters were not college graduates and when higher education was not very newsworthy. Times have changed. Higher education is news, and most reporters today have a B.A. and often an M.A. in journalism. They know about academia and love the smell of something fishy. We expect, and with justifiable paranoia, that a casual remark from a reporter is not casual, that anything we say can and will be used in evidence against us, that we are a possible source of news — and with luck, the road to a Pulitzer. No wonder, when I sit at my desk and blow my nose, I hope I am doing so photogenically.

This applies to all institutions, and their bosses, not just universities. To be in a prominent position today is to feel like you may be auditioning for the next sitcom called "University Exposure" or "State Department in a State" or something too grim to imagine. Institutions, and their leader-managers, are simply interesting to people. And in a never-stopping news cycle, the appetite the media have for anything that can pass as news is insatiable.

There is some advantage, however, in insatiable media. They want news, which allows you to make — or try to make — news on your own terms. In other words, a phone call from a university president or a government official or a company president is not extraordinary. Reporters are used to hearing from us and, in fairness to them, will give us a hearing. It may be our good news is not news at all to them, but we at least have the easy access to reporters, which gives us a chance to get some favorable coverage. Of course, if there is a whiff of the possibly unsavory behind the glowing good news, so much the better.

And that leads me to another, though recent, historical example of leadership and management. Again, this may surprise you because the example is President Bill Clinton. His limitations and bad personal judgment are well known — and a pity. But he has some lessons to teach us about the contemporary leader-manager.

First, he is a good reader, in other words, a constant student. Clinton is famous for whizzing through piles of documents, extracting what he needs to know, and hanging on to the information, organizing, and using it to great effect

His appearance early in 2000 before the Indian parliament is a case in point. While the press was beginning to write him off as a lame duck who was doing little more than shilling for his wife's senatorial campaign, Clinton managed to convince his Indian audience, a group that has often distrusted America, that he was probably a disciple of Gandhi and he had the facts about India's economy and geopolitical positions under his full control. He was a smash.

His study beforehand contributed to his success. His charm, which we all know about, helped. His projection of empathy was important. His understanding that he was in a public, that is to say a media, event also helped. He was there as a flesh-and-blood man, not a symbol. Here, not remote.

Those are the qualities history has discerned in Alexander and Charlemagne and Peter the Great. Those are the qualities I have discerned in the decidedly unheroic leader-managers of my experience and acquaintance. And those qualities combine often enough, I

think, for us to dispose of the proposal — or let me say the notion — that the two of them are antithetical. I believe leadership and management are not antonyms, but synonyms. Or, if they are not quite synonymous, they live together harmoniously in those of us who are willing to cultivate both qualities equally.

I have, I realize, referred to "prominent people" or "the boss" as I have been speaking to you. To leave you with the impression that I believe leadership and management combine only in the chief of the tribe would be a terrible error on my part. Were that the case, there would never be enough of each to go around, in the simplest of organizations to say nothing of the large and complex ones. If, for example, Lee Iaccoca had been the only person at Chrysler who could lead or manage, it never would have survived long enough for him to rise to the top — and to help save it once it began falling. Middle managers, people often referred to dismissively, make most organizations work — the way sergeants make the army work. The good ones manage, but they lead at the same time. Leadership, after all, does not require a big following. As far as that is concerned, one or two followers will do. But leadership requires vision, an understanding of where one wants to go and an equal understanding of how to get there.

That vision and understanding need to combine with management's greatest virtue, which is "an infinite capacity for taking pains." The famous phrase, written in 1870 by Jane Ellice Hopkins, was actually her definition of *genius*. But to marry that infinite capacity with vision and understanding looks very much like genius to me.

Looking Down, Around, and Ahead: Thoughts on the Management of Higher Education

SINCE MY TOPIC is higher education management, I have been asking myself what it is about this particular line of work that is different from other kinds of management, and what are its own special qualities. The results of this meditation provide me with three major questions:

- Can higher education be managed in any real sense?

- If so, what qualities are demanded of a person who seeks to be a higher education manager — a phrase, by the way, which I will simplify by referring to university presidents?

- What conclusions can we draw about the directions higher education management will be taking in the 21st century?

The answer to the first question must be *Yes*. It is so because higher education is functioning and, indeed, flourishing in the United States and in most countries of the world. The clamor for

Speech to faculty and students of Al-Akhawayn University in Ifrane, Morocco, March 9, 1999

admissions to colleges, universities, and graduate programs is loud and worldwide. But it is a *Yes* with footnotes, appendices, and an extensive critical apparatus. Some of that apparatus follows as the rest of my thoughts today.

If higher education can be managed, the qualities demanded of the manager or university president are special. Higher education has a character of its own. No other organization, to the best of my knowledge, includes so many *experts*, each of whom knows a great deal about a highly specialized field. The expert may be an economist or a chemist or a psychologist or an engineer. But what all experts have in common is *expertise*. This in turn makes them resistant to anything that looks or feel like management — that is, something that questions or even overrides their authoritative expertise. Someone once said to me that managing a knowledgeable faculty is akin to herding cats.

University presidents, like me, have adapted to such resistance in a number of ways in order to make it possible to manage their schools. One, of course, is simple internal politics. The president spends many hours speaking with or writing to those who are being managed. He struggles to convince them that a certain proposed policy is a good idea which will improve the lives of the faculty and make the whole school better, more stable, and perhaps wealthier. The faculty must understand, and appreciate, that the president of the university has many constituents, all of whom want something and who may not care if it comes at the expense of someone else. Persuasion is important, but so is patience.

Simple politics of this kind is seldom enough. In America, the university president also tries to establish a good relationship with the media — print, broadcast, and Internet. He needs to be on friendly terms with the reporters who cover the school. He needs to be friends with political figures who exercise some control over, or influence, his actions. And he answers every letter from either individual citizens, political figures, members of the faculty, students, and parents. He always stands ready to answer questions that come in over the telephone, sometimes at three in the morning or in the

middle of dinner with the family. He needs to be both the minister for foreign affairs and, an excellent public information staff notwithstanding, the university's chief flack.

Some of this may seem strange to you. Why, you might ask, should one bother so much cultivating the media when the people you are dealing with are mainly faculty? The answer, of course, is that the same professors also read the papers and watch television, and are more likely to favor a policy that seems to be receiving praise from those in no way connected with the school. Moreover, they too, like the university president, may have friends and influence in the media.

But there is much other work for the university president to do. There are, for example, faculty who never come into contact with me, but with one of my university's vice presidents or deans. Each of these officials needs to be encouraged to reinforce what I am doing through my own efforts. I stress "encouraged." They have a great deal of authority on their own, and I need to manage them so that faculty members feel that they are dealing with an academic administration that is consistent in its thinking and analysis of the problem at hand. The temptation can be to micromanage — to look over the shoulders of the vice presidents and deans. That strangles progress. That is why a university president must encourage his vice presidents and deans and stay in close enough contact — though without stifling them — to see that we are in agreement.

What the university president is struggling to accomplish, then, is the governance of a dynamic republic, a representative and, sometimes unruly, democracy. The problem is an *apparent* loss of authority by the faculty. Professors who are authorities in their fields don't like to feel that their university's president has authority over *them*. In America, faculties often talk about shared governance — shared between the faculty and administration — as if a thousand or two thousand professors would seriously take part, with one university president and a few other officials, in making major decisions. Moreover, few faculty members are inclined to make the kinds of *swift* decisions that have become more necessary, even in academic life, as a result of new technologies.

As Winston Churchill said, "democracy is the worst form of government except for all those other forms that have been tried from time to time." So what I am trying to accomplish is an exercise in representative democracy. That is admittedly not easy because, despite all the consultations with faculty and others, the final word comes from the administration, usually the president, and so the abstract "administration" or the concrete president — some would say "blockhead" — will appear to be both the source and the authority for the statement. The conclusion that might seem natural to draw is that managing a university or college is one of the most difficult jobs of administration ever invented. I feel reluctant to embrace that conclusion. The reason for my reluctance is that there are people for whom this work is a way of life or an old habit, but also a pleasurable, if challenging, business.

For example, my work allows me to deal with professors who are knowledgeable on many subjects that are not my specialty. On a typical day, I have the opportunity to learn all kinds of new things that enrich my professional and personal lives. I also have the pleasure of working on behalf of a university the foundations of which go back to George Washington, our first president. He had an idea for what he called "a national university." The living bloom of that idea is my school, The George Washington University. While not daring to compare myself to Washington, I can at least flatter myself that I am continuing his work.

So, a couple of conclusions before I turn to the future. I have already said that management of higher education is possible because we are functioning — and functioning well. My second conclusion is more complex. Higher education management offers some unique challenges which I have mentioned, but I doubt it is worse than, or completely different from, managing other sorts of institutions. Its own problems are counterbalanced by a range of its own pleasures that we must consider when we discuss this subject.

Moreover, I believe that the best university presidents feel a genuine admiration for faculty members who are doing important research — and an equal admiration for the university itself. Such a

manager ought to be capable of saying with complete sincerity, "If I were not the president of this university, then I would like to be a researcher and a teacher *here.*"

Since I am drawing conclusions, I will take my third question — what will university management be like in the future? — and answer it now. The answer is: it will be more difficult in some ways, easier in others. Here's why I think so:

Some things have changed for the better or at least the easier. University presidents no longer have to explain patiently to the public or anyone else the importance of higher education. A generation ago, in the United States, selling the virtues and values of higher education was one of our main activities. Now the public — and legislators — are convinced of the worth of higher education because of studies showing that university graduates have larger incomes, more satisfying careers, and even better health than those without it.

On the other hand, a university president is likely to be *made to feel* that he is really dispensing a public service. He is likely to hear that a university education should be available to all. But that is not the case, because universities are not dispensing water and electricity. In other words, the great and comparatively new faith in higher education has fed a notion that it is a commodity, endlessly and cheaply available. So, when the media ask the president why his school does not admit everyone who would like to attend, he needs to explain patiently that education costs money, that even professors expect to be paid for their work, and that the school is admitting as many *qualified* students as it can afford to admit and can accommodate in its classrooms. It is education, not a commodity.

Or is it? A challenge from another direction poses the question from a different perspective. Developments in information technology are allowing more and more American schools to offer courses and programs over the Internet. This has effectively disconnected the school, which does the teaching, from its geography. Thus, the school may be in Washington while students may be five or six thousand miles away in Alaska or Hawaii. Yet the student is able to be *at* the university

by turning on a computer. Does this mean that education — like ordering a sweater or a book online — *has* become a commodity?

I think not. But I hasten to add that online education is becoming so common that it has begun to influence how university presidents think of themselves and their schools. We all worry, for example, that schools have begun to produce entirely different kinds of graduates, even if their records and papers look the same.

The first group, those who actually studied on campus, met other students, benefited from the give-and-take in classrooms or over lunch, breathed in the social and cultural atmosphere of the university. They were part of a community. And if the university's campus was in a city like Boston or New York or Washington or San Francisco, these students were also exposed to a cultural feast from which they will certainly profit for the rest of their lives.

The second group of students, meanwhile, studied elsewhere. They may have learned as much in purely academic terms — although even here, it is harder to measure accomplishment and progress at long range. But beyond this, managers worry, have they benefited as much in broader *human* terms? Are they as sophisticated? As well spoken? As adult in their behavior? As capable as the first group of engaging in rational disagreement and rational defense of their own ideas? Some of them, after all, may have been sitting in a room for four years without ever having human contact with a professor or a fellow student.

This is troublesome, but the fact is that this kind of learning is here to stay. We are moving toward a computer explosion of such magnitude that shortly, in America, it will be a rare person who does not own, or cannot get quick access to, a computer and the Internet. In addition to what I have just said about the social and human qualities of education, there will be something else for us in higher education to consider.

Imagine, for example, that a university is offering a course in the history of North Africa. Imagine that, of the 20 students enrolled in the course, five are actually visiting Morocco, four are taking the

course over the Internet, six are doing research on North African history in European universities, and the remaining five are actually sitting in classrooms on the university campus.

The first question is this: have all 20 really taken the same course? From different places and from different perspectives, they may all have benefited, but in very different ways. If they were all equally good ways, there would be little troubling doubt. But that, I fear, is unlikely — and how would we ever know?

Then begin the kind of headaches that no manger wants. How much should students from these different groups pay for the course? What role should the course play in the student's overall academic record? How do we pay for the information technology needed? And that's the simple part.

Should a student who actually visited Morocco demand reduced tuition payments because he placed fewer demands on university services and uncovered data which the university will be able to use in future courses? Should a student who visits Morocco *and* Algeria also get some preference or even a stipend? Such talk of money may appear unseemly to you — it often does to me — but I hear it often. A student who traveled and has to pay as much tuition as a student who stayed on the university campus may grow angry. A student who studied at home may feel the same way. Both are capable of making their grievances public, in the media, presenting the university as unfair, unfeeling, and unfriendly.

I confess I am not sure how to manage all this. I don't mean just the protests about money but also the management of the quality of education and its results. This is new and in many ways exciting. But we would lose something, in fact, cheapen something that has acquired greater and greater value over the years if we let it become a commodity. Education is not that. I suspect, optimistically, that the next generation of university presidents, vice presidents, and deans will have a better sense of information technology as a partner of education. They will have grown up with it and will take it as customary, certainly more than people of my generation have.

And that is really the final lesson about managing a college or a university. We may expect that the governance and the technology we have grown more or less used to in recent years will never reach what physicists call a steady state. Something will constantly — and predictably — tip things off balance. The real challenge is to manage these changes with a sense of poise that brings the university back constantly — and predictably — to a point of equilibrium.

External Expectations
for Campus Leaders

AH, THE HAZARDS of the Luncheon Keynote! No sooner do I agree to talk about "External Expectations for Campus Leaders" than another idea begins to shove it aside. So how, I wonder, would a speech on "America as a College-Educated Society" sound? Probably something like this.

When I talk about a college-educated America, I don't mean a nation where everyone has been graduated from a four-year program. But I do mean an America where so many people have attended college that we have created an academic culture that is now familiar to nearly every citizen.

America's colleges and universities are now firmly established as part of our national life and national economy. What we do and decide on campus is important off campus — in government offices and businesses and the media, especially in the media. That has raised the expectations people have of campus leaders and of higher education. The interest is intense everywhere you look. The smallest newspapers in the smallest towns show no less interest in reporting on the new community college or the average board scores of their

Speech to the American Council on Education's Fellows Program awards luncheon, June 8, 2001

high school students than the big-market papers and TV stations show in reporting on Harvard or Columbia or, naturally, The George Washington University.

Half a century ago, this wasn't the case. Colleges were news around commencement time, mainly because the guest speaker was interesting and not because the local media — or anyone not attached to the school — cared about a sweaty procession of rented black robes. In a college-educated society, the interest is year long. The media people are nearly all college educated now, many with a master's in journalism. The university's neighbors are more likely than not to be college educated, and to have an opinion about what the school is up to and how it is behaving. Only a very dense administrator can fail to notice, and to understand, that a university is a treasury of stories waiting to happen, and often not stories that the administrator, or the board of trustees, would like to see in print.

This kind of public attention and high expectation is good in some ways, not so good in others. It is good because our society is finally paying attention to its institutions of higher learning. This attention tends to be a useful corrective to the ivory tower. It also tugs universities toward better citizenship. If big corporations can talk about being "good corporate citizens" — and often even do something to prove it — why shouldn't universities do the same? They breathe the same air as their fellow citizens, drink the same water, travel on the same streets. The public's heightened interest in us pays off well in making us more interested in them.

The same intense interest in universities, however, is not always for the good. Some of it — frequently, I think, too much of it — is simply looking for trouble, looking to find one of those bad campus stories just waiting to be told, waiting to watch the mighty fall. We often call this "gotcha journalism" though the attitude is shared by many outside the media. And, to be sure, universities are not the only targets. If you have any doubts, ask Gary Hart ... if you can find him these days.

Perhaps that's the price of our success. When you and I were growing up, the word "education" without an adjective in front of it meant primary and secondary schools. "College" was a possibility that got tucked away at the end of a long sentence, if mentioned at all. It was a remote possibility for most. The shoe is on the other foot today: Primary and secondary education are often seen as preludes to *real education*, which begins with the freshman year in college and may end with a graduate degree or two.

In light of these changes, campus leaders, from presidents on down, have watched their roles change. They may still be ceremonial figures who pour a fine dry sherry, but the ceremony and the sherry get squeezed into a very busy life. Presidents raise money. Presidents do public relations. Presidents serve as the image of the institution, not in ceremonies, but often live on camera. And the same is true of the other administrators.

This new and complex presidential role provoked protests that boomed like the broadsides at the battle of Trafalgar. But the cannon balls, I am glad to say, fell into the water and sank. A great transition had taken place. An expanded, and expansive, college and university system was clearly serving an expanding national economy and increasingly unified national culture, thanks to TV, cheap long-distance, and the Internet. The president's role had to expand to keep pace. Many of us feel we are on call, if not on duty, 24/7. We are.

We have seen a redefinition of our functions We must deal, on shorter and shorter notice, with many off-campus constituencies including business, government, the courts, the medical profession, even the Immigration and Naturalization Service. An academically minded president may insist that only the school's own commitments should guide his or her actions. But others who claim a stake in the university see it otherwise. It is an inevitable debate — and one the university president cannot really win — because the entire academic establishment has been quite thoroughly integrated into the world's most productive and powerful society. Good and not so good, as I said before. But it is a fact.

I myself am a representative fact of this integration. I am not an academic by training, but a lawyer. Time was, that would have been an unlikely qualification — more likely, a disqualification — for the job. But as colleges and universities became more sensitive to the possibilities of "big trouble" on campus, more alert to the various pitfalls that unthinking but apparently discriminatory policies prepared for them, and more conscious of the media's hunger for a good and preferably scandalous story, they began to hanker for lawyers to sit on the top of the pyramid.

It wouldn't hurt if the lawyer had some actual courtroom experience. A combination of combativeness and advocacy was welcome. Still is. Nor would it hurt if the president had the habit of reviewing books or had been a talking head on television And if not a lawyer, a businessman or a retired politician might do.

And for good reason. No school wanted a chief administrator who was going to burn out in five or six years. When a destructive protest denounces a forum on racial prejudice as capitulation to gross colonialism and when the accompanying sit-in becomes a campus riot, suitable for live coverage by TV helicopters, you certainly want a president who, in cardiac arrest, can compose his face with just the right hints of determination and humor as he is loaded into the ambulance.

Well, I jest ... a little. The kind of toughness a president needs can exist in a classical scholar or a physicist as well as in a lawyer. But the toughness is the point. By that, I don't mean a mean spirit or a bad temper or an autocratic rule. I mean a durability and an infinite patience, even in the face of a complete, and sometimes willful, misunderstanding of what a university is. Let me give you a couple of examples.

It comes out from time to time that a university has a public relations department, though it may have some other name. What's this? Public relations in a college? I sent my kids there so they would be smart enough to see through public relations types. What are you doing? Well, what we are doing is simple. We are telling our story. We are presenting our strengths — and, if we have any sense, we will admit our weaknesses and fix them. We have public relations for the same

reason any other institution has public relations — because people who are heartily interested in us may not have our interests at heart.

Another example. University lawyers had to admit *in court* that their schools actually owned real estate. And they sometimes earned big bucks from their real estate. To measure the extent of the shock these revelations caused, let me ask you to think historically. The academic sector is an heir to the charity sector — because the clerics who staffed the first universities in the Middle Ages taught and wrote for the sake of God, not Mammon. No matter that the 13th century universities were *not* free, and did not have campus police and dining halls and residences and library collections that would have made the monks swoon.

Yet another example. Had the university's school of engineering really signed a research contract with the Air Force? Well, then, no missile ever fired went faster and straighter to its target than the missives fired by protesters at the university in question.

How can things like these — public relations, ownership of real estate, military contracts, and many other things — be consistent with humane studies? How could we do such awful things? The answer is simple. We have *always* done all kinds of things, *always* claimed to harbor knowledge about everything in the universe, *always* did things that someone thought perfectly awful and unworthy of a university. There has *always* been, in any good university, the risk of appearing incoherent or contradictory. The risk arose from latent to visible as the universities themselves became more visible.

Thus the rising interest in universities has brought risk as well as pleasure — and managing them both now is really the most daunting job administrators face. A university has always been a center for accumulating and dispensing knowledge. There is nothing exceptionable in that — unless the knowledge becomes an instrument of power in the hands of an academic Svengali. Of course, universities have been accused of that, especially in cases of what we used to elegantly call *moral turpitude*, otherwise known as sex with students.

But the power of the university's store of knowledge outside the campus has done our schools a power of good. The post-war expansion of the United States created a demand for academic experts, authorities, and gurus. Professors off to Washington to testify before Congress or advise the secretary of state were good press releases for us and just plain good press. Academic glamour was really a sword with two edges.

First, it enabled us to say that we were not residents of an ivory tower. The fellow with chalk on his sleeve in front of the blackboard may have just come back from a chalk talk with the president ... of the United States or even — dare I say the name? — General Motors. Second, every image or story about a professor heading off to Geneva or Delhi or Lagos was in effect an advertisement, more expressive and less expensive than any we could devise or pay for ourselves. Such a story or picture suggested that to be an undergraduate here was to mingle with the great and to be on the way up, right into the American ruling class.

In short, if I had to name the most important academic development of the 20th century, I could do a lot worse than to say it was the steady and pervasive *integration* of the academy with America itself. The early 20th century saw conservative universities replenishing a small group of leaders in politics and business. As the century ended, the academy was turning out leaders in every imaginable field — not replenishing a tiny elite, but creating an enormous new one: college-educated America. As a convenient symbol of this expanded role, consider that President George W. Bush, admittedly part of the elite old guard, is the first American president to have an M.B.A. I hasten to add that Secretary of State Colin Powell, who certainly didn't have a silver spoon, also holds an M.B.A. — from The George Washington University.

Integrating the academy with America and integrating the schools themselves — along racial, class, and intellectual lines — have proved, like almost everything else I have observed today, to be mixed blessings. The radical students of the 1960s and even later have found fault with our policies and attitudes — and when we have negotiated

with them, we have been accused from the outside of capitulation to outrageous demands or fostering nihilism, even anti-Americanism. When we have done business with business or the military, we have been excoriated from the inside for selling out or selling our souls. It sounds like sailing between Scylla and Charybdis, but we — all of us, or at least most of us — have not run up on the rocks and foundered. The price of this complex integration is a certain amount of chaos.

But chaos, like the apparent incoherence of universities that I mentioned a little earlier, is probably healthy. It brews things up, and some of those things are good. It takes us in new and promising directions. But that leads me to a question. What does all this that I have been describing amount to? Can we expect more of the same in the future? Will we continue, amid the chaos, to find new and fresh ways of connecting with college-educated America? Or should we expect to see changes of a completely different nature?

To find a plausible answer to this question, I propose looking at the Internet. We hear that the Internet can, and will soon, abolish the idea of education on a university campus. Knowledge being free and free-flowing on the Internet, this argument runs, makes bricks and mortar, not to mention professors and presidents, obsolete or at least implausible. That's another way of saying our students do not need guidance and can manage the hit-or-miss intellectual qualities of the Internet on their own.

If you believe the university is at present a great big pipe with a bunch of funnels at one end for spooning out knowledge, then the Internet as replacement looks likely. Both are mechanisms, devices. But the chaos of the campus challenges this image. Lively debate and even turbulent disagreement and protest animate the academic process. This animation will not flow from the Internet any more than it ever flowed out of a pipe full of porridge.

We send our children to college so they can make their way in our society. That implies, among other things, the ability to manage themselves in debate and discussion, to reason, to develop a healthy skepticism. They may learn many things on the Internet — GW certainly

uses it and encourages its use. But learning how to put what they learn to good use, to profit from the information and knowledge that add up to an education, will never, I believe, come out of a mechanism or a device. It is much more likely to grow out of a calm and a personal resilience that turbulence and even chaos can nurture.

To put it plainly, we teach facts *and* we teach how to deal with facts. We teach techniques *and* how to use techniques. We teach great thoughts *and* how to think. We teach the *how* because education does not end with a degree in hand. The facts, techniques, and thoughts may change or be disproven or discarded, but how to deal with facts, how to use techniques, and how to think are constant.

These would be good expectations for colleges and universities to have for ourselves. And equally good expectations for those outside the university to have for us. Nor do I think this is really more of same — another name for what we have been doing all along. I believe this because by teaching as I propose, we will be teaching something to college-educated America that constantly *refreshes* itself, that is *not* the same. We will be teaching what it feels like to be educated, to feel conflict inside oneself and to resolve the conflict, to be, simply, sophisticated. It is a very high expectation.

Treating American Mood Swings

PUBLIC ADMINISTRATION is a funny kind of business and so, in its own way, is business administration. Nothing's very funny about what these disciplines are as courses of study or professions. But they are seen in a funny light — or rather, the American public suffers from violent mood swings about what we study and what we do.

On the one hand, it is a generally recognized triumph that we now award a masters in public administration. It has raised the concept of administering a public function from the realm of mere politics to the realm of professionalism. Whoever runs the water supply of a major city no longer has as a primary credential a blood-relation to the mayor. The most naïve members of our citizenry today want their public administrators to look like members of the same general species as their doctors and lawyers.

Business administration is in pretty much the same position. As is inevitably the case, the existence of the M.B.A. degree has led to a kind of standardization that makes instant sense out of the statements "She has an M.B.A." and "She *doesn't* have an M.B.A." Few parents doubt a

Speech to students in the GW Masters of Public Administration and Masters of Business Administration Associations, September 9, 1999

child stands a good chance of earning a better salary in the corporate world with a degree that guarantees some familiarity with the business issues of finance, marketing, production, and sales.

But on the other hand — there are always two — on the *inevitable* other hand, the triumph of these two fields, and especially public administration, sometimes looks like just the opposite. Strange, but I said it is seen in a funny light. This is especially the case when we are dealing with a public mood that is so powerfully — and often unreflectively — anti-government. You are just as likely these days to hear Democrats as well as Republicans decrying "big government" and hoping to reduce the power, influence, and prerogatives of local, state, and national governments. "Free enterprise," as we all seem to have been convinced, is the magic answer to the awful horrors of swollen, bloated, dysfunctional, top-down government, all of which we have inherited in parts here and there from Genghis Khan, Ivan the Terrible, and Joseph Stalin.

A mood like this is difficult to fight because it seems capable of instant amnesia, but not of logic. Look these advocates of less government in the face and remind them that even the simplest aspects of our daily life — the water supply, traffic lights, highway repairs, safe food, among dozens and hundreds of other things — must obviously be regulated and that regulation implies government. Do this, and you risk being looked at in your term as one of the last surviving members of the American Communist Party.

Meanwhile, would-be business administrators are likely to encounter a similar phenomenon. They are likely to hear someone assert that a high school education and a lot of entrepreneurial drive are all you really need to flourish in modern business. Protest this view, and you are likely to be met with the triumphant question, "What about Bill Gates?" Or the observation that neither J.P. Morgan nor Andrew Carnegie held an M.B.A.

These arguments ignore, of course, the obvious. One is that Gates may not have an M.B.A., but once Microsoft became a business,

he was pretty quick to start hiring M.B.A.s, many of whom deserve a great deal of the credit for the success of Microsoft.

It is just as obvious that the study of business administration helps us to see if the lessons taught by the careers of Morgan and Carnegie can be taught to a large audience and still have anything to teach us. A study of how they managed their businesses will reveal how different business practices are today. Tell an audience today that, to avert a crash in the American economy, Alan Greenspan and Bob Rubin are going to meet in the private mansion of a modern-day J.P. Morgan — and the economy is likely to crash on the instant of that news. What saved us once would destroy us today.

So, we face a certain challenge as we try to reconcile our country to our degrees and our careers. The fear of tyranny goes back to the founding of the country. Read the 10 amendments that make up the Bill of Rights, and what you see is a list of prohibitions on Congress, a fundamental limiting of government power. Talk to Americans about anarchy and disorder, and they are likely to shift the conversation to the perils of too much government, of snooping, of prying, of lack of privacy. Then ask them if they would like the pediatrician who cares for their kids *not* to have a license to practice medicine recognized by the state. Perhaps they will answer that a free enterprise situation is likely to provide more effective regulation than some "czar" who sits in an office and couldn't cure a cocker spaniel of ringworm. It's a dim argument, but it certainly avoids the issue or rather seems to forget it entirely. Amnesia, as I said before.

In short, those who are working toward the M.P.A. or the M.B.A. are dealing not only with the issue of education but also with the issue of love. Our country seems to be out of love with you. So, we need to figure out ways of appealing not just to its head — which is hard enough — but to its heart.

And what better place to begin than in our elementary schools? We claim to be teaching kids the basics. By common consent, these include reading, writing, and arithmetic as well as some knowledge of history, geography, and what is sometimes called social studies.

Shouldn't it also include some courses that help answer questions like these? For example:

- How do I know that the water in the faucet isn't poisonous?

- Why don't we get sick from food we buy in the supermarket?

- If somebody shoots my dad in North Carolina, why can't that person just move to South Carolina and stay out of trouble?

- Who checks the stairs in front of my school to make sure they're not falling down?

- This is a free country, so how come someone can tell us to drive at 60 miles per hour when I want to go 90?

- If deadly snakes are working their way into the lake where we go swimming, is there someone in charge of getting them out?

- And maybe best of all, whose job is it to think up questions like these in the first place?

Don't laugh. Just put yourself in the shoes of a child who has simply gotten used to the idea that there's always pure water in the faucet and the traffic lights always work. The notion that our large and complex society requires non-stop supervision and maintenance is suddenly a brand-new discovery, as novel as some revelation about reading, writing, and arithmetic.

Moreover, an awareness of public administration in many ways puts a finishing touch on the study of American history and society. The Europeans who first arrived in North America found a world where public administration — in our sense — was unnecessary. Being few in number at first, their initial excesses did little harm. But years and centuries of pillage and ecological malpractice led their descendents to realize that their environment was not in fact infinite and self-healing. If we did not want a wasteland, we were going to set up public authorities whose mission was preservation rather than limitless development. The resulting structure we now take for granted.

Another example. Read a little about what Americans of the 19th century put into their stomachs and veins — and the stomachs and veins of their children. It took a new generation of physicians and a regulatory agency, the Food and Drug Administration, to banish the snake-oil cures and guaranteed "remedies for the female problems" that in many cases were toxic and in the rest simply did no good at all. To learn things like this would surely be of benefit to children trying to make sense of the world.

They could also benefit from a systematic approach to learning about how businesses are administered. To have a look at the Coca-Cola Company after years of drinking Coke is to locate yourself, for the first time, in the American marketplace, as the target of a major marketing effort. It also is to begin to conceive of the American corporate universe as a place with jobs to offer — or decline — and a place where one could use one's talents.

Some people, of course, would say this is not education but a spoiling of childhood. Leave the kids in blissful ignorance of the intricate systems of public and business administration, they warn us. Wasn't it the New Left that sought the same kind of disenchantment and disaffection? Who needs it?

I have a little more faith than that in the intelligence of our kids. They watch TV, hear some news on the car radio perhaps, or get on the Internet, so they will scarcely be in a delightful state of enchantment, convinced that the planet Earth is really the earthly paradise. What we would be doing, if we exposed them to the rudiments of administration, is in fact giving them some reasons for hope and some defenses against despair. After all, if the Coke bottles don't reach the supermarket shelves by divine magic, then maybe what's inside the Coke bottle has something to do with human decision, human influence, and human intervention. That your mom and dad are petitioning the town to get a traffic light installed at the corner where your friend was almost hit by a car three days ago is a process that will surely seem clearer once you have got some picture of the governing authority that runs a typical American town.

I'm sure it's obvious to you that I am calling for a change in the American consciousness of what an education is. It must take into account the training and practice of business and public administration as forces that help shape American life. And as must be equally obvious, such a change in consciousness inevitably carries political overtones. Will today's Americans really sit still if we suggest that government not only *isn't* sinful by nature but is often absolutely necessary? That administration is not tyranny, but simply planning, accounting, producing, and *imagining*?

In other words, such additions to our elementary schools' curricula will definitely be perceived as "controversial." They will be argued over long and furiously. They will bounce across the pages of our newspapers and TV networks. And only when the kids exposed to these changes actually turn out to be doing better in college and in their jobs is the argument likely to be settled in favor of the new. So, I counsel patience.

I think resistance like this has something to do with a latent, but widespread, fear of anarchy, a companion to its fear of tyranny. I'm not sure I know where it comes from. The Founders seemed to believe that an educated and free public, especially an educated and free electorate, was a guarantee of order. I agree with them. Yet it seems today that people who can think for themselves — who are educated and free — are surely only a step away from rebellion, *armed* rebellion, thanks to the Second Amendment.

As people who spend a lot of time at a university, we should be — and, I think, are — well armed to reply to fears like these. If there's one thing our history and sociology courses aim to do, it is to get their students to think critically and seriously about American life. But we have yet to hear that college graduates are the potential leaders of an armed insurrection that will overthrow the existing order of the United States. Indeed, look at the rhetorical violence of the '60s and '70s, and then look at their consequences — a continuing neoconservatism the peaks of which we are still learning to scale. The people who do not think critically, the militia types in northern

Idaho, are the truly dangerous people and more likely than anyone to promote anarchy and armed rebellion.

Meanwhile, as next year's presidential election draws closer, education is on everybody's mind. Al Gore has called for nothing less than a "revolution" in how our public schools instruct our children. Education is on George W. Bush's lips as frequently. But what is lacking from the candidates is a clear statement of how our present system of education should be modified in order to serve the real needs of America in the new century.

No clear statement and no national consensus is likely to develop until we begin to envision a system that does three things:

- ♦ Prepares our children more effectively and realistically for the challenges they will face in developing careers that are stimulating and useful, as well as financially rewarding.

- ♦ Is not so obsessed with *order* that it cannot tolerate a little disagreement between advocates of liberty and advocates of good function.

- ♦ Turns out the kind of graduates — from elementary school, middle school, and high school — who *don't* take things on faith.

But I do have enough faith myself to say that today's young people, including our university students, look like a group singularly given to calm and reason. They seem almost hysteria-proof. They're actually given to pondering rather than shouting. And they are good at quickly suppressing — usually through quiet humor or what they call "irony" — those among them who are likely to cause trouble. Who needs more hassles when you're trying to put together a life and a career in a world that spins as fast and furiously as the one we actually inhabit?

That calm, I truly believe, comes from thoughtfulness, not merely absorbed concentration on getting a job and making money. And if I am right in my belief, then it's a good omen that we are becoming more and more what I have always longed for America to be: an educated society where everyone has the right to vote and the right to think. And does both.

New

Ways

---

of

Thinking

Going Bipolar
in the Groves of Academe

WHEN YOU ARE THE PRESIDENT of a university in Washington, D.C., as I am, a funny thing happens to your professional life. You begin to get invitations to visit other countries and look at other cultures, all of them keenly interested in American higher education and how it works. You get to meet the presidents of these countries and their prime ministers and ministers of education. You talk to the presidents (or rectors or chancellors) of their universities.

And what you soon discover is what you had reason to know before you ever left home — that American colleges and universities are the subjects of international admiration, international emulation, and, sometimes, international wonder. You can imagine the pleasure that the peripatetic president feels in the glow of this praise and even envy.

Then, you return to the United States and read all the usual columns that deal with our country's system of higher education. Tuition is much too high, they all seem to agree, and American families are having a miserable time paying for their kids' education. But then, they continue, it doesn't matter anyway because our colleges

Speech to the Educational Testing Service/USIA Summit, entitled "U.S. Leadership in International Education: The Lost Edge?" on September 24, 1998

are teaching politically correct trash. Worse still, when they are not instructing the young in gay and lesbian themes in the Book of Deuteronomy, they are introducing them to a social history that blends Marx, Manichaean theology, and mushy leftovers of 1960s anti-American radicalism.

Having run into this experience several times, I've asked myself how to account for such a bipolar perspective of the American academy. Across our borders, across the pond, and on the far side of the globe the conversational tone is one of envious longing. If only we had a system like yours, they seem to say again and again, we could solve a lot of our problems. But at home, the tone is one of contempt and fatigue, as if to say, "Our system is totally degraded. Let's just cancel the whole enterprise and start over with a fresh spirit or just let the whole thing wither away because the Internet is going to put colleges and universities out of business anyway."

Individuals suffering from bipolar disorder can take medications. I doubt it's possible to dose the entire public, foreign and domestic, that has something to say about higher education. But having pondered this split for many years, I have arrived at several conclusions about how this bipolarity has come about and what we can do to treat it. In hopes that people will swallow them, I'll offer them up one at a time.

Conclusion Number One: *Many Americans are not aware that the eminent international standing of their higher education system is a result of American history, especially in the 20th century.*

I am thinking of my undergraduate years at Columbia College in New York. At the very apex of the pyramid of academic honors awarded to each graduating class were two scholarships, one sending a student to Oxford, the other to Cambridge. In other words, the greatest honor was to be shipped out of the country. These scholarships reflected a much broader phenomenon of the time — the degree of *anglophilia* that dominated the liberal arts faculties at a time when the study of the liberal arts was naturally taken to be the "core" of a college education. Standing right behind anglophilia was *europhilia*, the sense and sentiment

that a German or Italian university founded in the 13th or 14th century is ever so much older, wiser, deeper, and mellower than their American step-siblings which had been founded "only yesterday."

In those days, the envy was aimed by Americans at Western Europe with a particular affection for England. The *Times Literary Supplement*, published in London, was required reading for anyone teaching in the English Department, though the donnish and, in those days, anonymous reviews seemed to produce more score-settling than enlightenment. No matter. And a professor who announced that he was going to spend his summer in research at the British Museum had simply handed you his credentials as a serious scholar.

At the same time, faculty vied for grants that would allow them to travel to France and Italy, examining the ancient texts and artifacts of those lovely mellow civilizations while incidentally plunging into their infinitely lovelier and mellower cuisines and vineyards. America, even before McDonald's, was burgers and boiled dinners. Europe was three hours at the dinner table in Lyon or Bologna, complemented by the local wine which (alas!) did not travel and could only be appreciated on the spot. Could you even imagine dining like that in Atlanta or Des Moines?

This mid-20th-century sense of academic and cultural inferiority was deepened, especially in the Ivy League, by what I'll offer as the second of my conclusions.

Conclusion Number Two: *American higher education in the middle of the 20th century was influenced by a degree of class consciousness that prevented academics from taking seriously most of the higher education actually being dispensed in America at the time.*

Once the Ivy League schools got through boasting about their foundings in the 17th or 18th centuries, about having "turned out" the most important figures in American history, and about having in their rare book rooms manuscripts so precious that no human being would ever be allowed to see them, they barely had the time to give a perfunctory nod in the direction of all the other colleges and universities in the United States.

Some of them were enormous factories, which seemed to do something called football. They made movies about them. There were military academies, where the students marched from the parade ground to the classroom and back. We knew about these places from movies also. Others, according to rumors, were called "state" colleges and universities, from unheard of places. And then there were places called — unbelievably — "junior colleges," which appeared to be second-chance high schools for those who were at the bottom of the intellectual ladder and headed *down*. Later, calling them community colleges changed nothing.

The sheer snobbery that I am trying to describe is rather hard to recapture today. It was all bound up with tweed jackets, briar pipes, a sense of upper class entitlement, tradition, and a belief that the truly educated American was in truth a European put down through some blunder in an essentially barbaric nation. These sentiments, distant though they may seem today, were routine and taken for granted at the time. And they poured the foundation for my third conclusion.

Conclusion Number Three: *In a higher-education establishment largely ignorant of the American economy, the role of colleges and universities in our economic development was truly a non-subject.*

In a society where Alan Greenspan and Robert Rubin are pinups, you know the economy is front-page and pervasive news. The movements of the Dow, the status of our current accounts in imports and exports, and the local carburetor company's exploration of Central Asian markets all seem perfectly natural as newsworthy items. Half a century ago, for most of those teaching at a respectable college, these concerns were almost unheard of. A professor overheard talking about them was clearly a member of the economics department, which ranked well below Romance languages or Asian history. Actual discussion of something called *money* may even have marked its academic perpetrator as someone from the thing that called itself *the business school*, where grotesque subjects like advertising were taken seriously, no doubt to please some Republican on the board of trustees.

In and of itself, the bipolar state of mind that I've tried to describe amounted to a profound schism between the United States and its own system of higher education, especially among the schools at the head of the academic pecking order. There seems to have been a complete disconnect between how the colleges and universities saw themselves and what was going on, on the campuses of "other places" *and* on their own. And this had longer-term and even more serious consequences, as shown in my fourth and fifth conclusions, which I will present separately although they are related.

Conclusion Number Four: *The great anti-academic "rebellion" of the 1960s was aimed at a way of life that had already lost confidence in itself. The rebellion has since given way to a counter-rebellion so defensive in tone that it inclines to favor almost any institution which may be called "traditional" as opposed to "innovative," "unprecedented," or, God forbid, "revolutionary."*

When students on the east and west coasts launched their protests and sit-ins against the schools in which they were enrolled, they typically condemned them as temples of irrelevance, utterly disconnected from the realities of American life. You could learn more, they asserted, by walking through a nearby minority ghetto than from attending all the required freshman and sophomore courses.

What made these charges embarrassing, of course, was their element of truth. Not the whole truth, but the students had a point. There was no doubt value in a philosophy class on ethics to look at the differences in the idea of the Good in Plato, Bentham, and Hume. But ethical considerations also applied to daily life, whether in the nearby ghetto or in their own suburban neighborhoods. Moreover, in the postwar years students and faculty, including the establishment as well as the radical professors, had no idea where the money that supported their school was actually coming from. If you had told them that the United States was the international economic and industrial heavyweight, and that American manufacturers and exports raised the capital that enabled the federal and state governments to shower subsidies on the colleges and universities of

America, you would have seen only a very puzzled look. That thinking was not in fashion in the *academic* ghetto.

When the student rampages quickly attracted local and national media attention to their "cause," they soon found that their darts and arrows were drawing real blood. Administrators and professors, when confronted with a microphone, voiced the kind of bewilderment that seemed indistinguishable from personal ignorance. The complete absence of anyone with a dark skin on campus was obvious from even the most casual sweep of the TV camera. And for the first time, though certainly not the last, Americans got used to hearing that those on academic payrolls were being paid for *not* working, *not* functioning, and *not* measuring up, rather than for doing what most Americans did for their money, which was to work from nine to five 50 weeks a year.

The schools wanted to compensate for these failings, and predictably overcompensated. Required courses in the western humanities were dropped in favor of optional courses on, you could say, everything *but*. Students with dark skin and Hispanic surnames were recruited with the kind of energy previously reserved for football stars. Ethnic studies and courses on Third World virtue filled up while courses in Shakespeare and the Victorian novel emptied out.

When this compensation reached its predictable extreme, an academic counter-revolution, symbolized and spearheaded by the National Association of Scholars, was already tracking state by state the victories being won by "traditionalists" over the excesses of the "tenured radicals" who thought they hadn't done their duty until they had convinced their students to be thoroughly anti-American. It was hogwash, no more correct really than the hidebound snobbery it was trying to replace. And that leads me to the fifth and last conclusion that I want to offer.

Conclusion Number Five: *Americans do not see that our system of higher education has become the international model of how one goes about serving the needs of a modern industrial state and a modern liberal democracy.*

The controversies between the traditionalists and the radicals caused both sides infinite trouble in seeing what was right before them — even, as I have said, right on their own campuses. They did not realize that what they did for American students aroused admiration and even envy in the rest of the world. While some students supported by generous scholarships or well-heeled parents studied in foreign universities or took their junior year abroad, students from everywhere else in the world poured into American classrooms. Meanwhile, political and cultural leaders abroad studied American higher education precisely because it was such a pervasive system and so obviously and profoundly tied to American economic development.

And I really do mean pervasive. No matter where you live in this country, you are rarely if ever very far from a community college or state college of some kind. Enter one of them and you have set foot on the grand staircase at the top of which stand the Ivy League schools and their many domestic competitors. And we are all familiar with the good results of this upward academic mobility. The local factory can find the employees it needs to run its increasingly computerized operations. Companies seeking certification in different skills can turn to community colleges for dependable programs — programs which typically enroll people long out of school, but who realize more than many academics that "lifelong learning" is a real thing. And the biggest of corporations can choose their young managers from the graduates of a host of business schools, the world's finest, judging by the number of foreign students they enroll.

Without this decentralized system of higher education, American productivity, American wealth, and American living standards would be nowhere near where they are today. I do not believe that the sole and justifying point of education is to power the economy. But without pervasive higher education, our economy and our lives would both be lesser than they are now.

I am often tempted to call what we have "The University of the United States." Typically American, this mega-school is decentralized yet voluntarily manages to keep its thousands of parts integrated and interchangeable so that a community college graduate from Illinois can readily go on to earn a B.A. in Los Angeles, and an

M.B.A. or Ph.D. in Texas, then snag a first job in Virginia or Colorado. And this integration extends to the professoriat, especially in the research universities, where professors variously and widely serve as consultants, advisors, consciences, gadflies, and analysts of our manufactures, intellectual property, politics, and entertainment.

I think it's true to say that the United States is now part of our higher education system as much as higher education is part of the United States. Perhaps the rise of the Internet and the global economic dependence on the flow of information made this inevitable. But I think it is important to observe, as I have tried through these five conclusions, that America got there first even if American universities themselves weren't the first to realize it. Even when the Ivies were still fixated on Oxford and Cambridge, American colleges were already supporting the postwar American economy in ways that stimulated further development and moved the United States toward its present status as the only global superpower.

It is time for America to catch up — with itself. It is time to start treating our bipolar disorder. Some colleges are party schools, but most are not sinks of debauchery or crash courses in the Seven Deadly Sins. There remain politically correct, and academically bankrupt, courses, but the rigors in science courses and economics, to name just two examples, should be a point of pride for students, faculty, administrators, and every last citizen among us.

And we will catch up with ourselves if we catch up with what the rest of the world already knows: From the founding of Harvard in 1636 to the creation of a community college last week, "The University of the United States" has moved from strength to strength. And one last, and happy, thought: Our colleges and universities show every sign of growing even more robust, more critical to our well being, and more admired. I hope some of that admiration now begins at home.

When Your Culture Operates on Your Brain

AS THE PRESIDENT of a large university, I'm asked to keep track of a rather broad array of ideas, ranging from the earth-shaking to the somewhat dubious. It can be exhausting, but it gets to be a habit. And my habit has just recently retrieved this thought from the ideas grab bag that I always seem to have my hand in.

It seems to me that our world has been making a gigantic and rather dismaying change in its most basic thought processes, a change that's been going on for some 40 years and that affects the lives of everybody in this room.

To grasp this change and its scope, think back to the world about 40 years ago. That world, the world of 1958, spent a lot of time marveling at how fast things were starting to move. Jet planes were breaking the sound barrier. Television was bringing us pictures from the scene of the crime — or at least the political convention. And television had brought about its media revolution with the speed of a zapping Hollywood cartoon. The postal service was offering hints that the division between regular mail and air mail was becoming

Speech to the Rotary Club of Friendship Heights, Washington, D.C., October 29, 1998

obsolete. Regular mail, to move faster, would move by air. And we were getting used to the notion that we would soon be flying to Europe for a long weekend and get back on the job without missing a day.

"Things are moving so fast these days!" That was a statement — nowadays, we'd call it a mantra — we heard over and over again 40 years ago. But even as they moved faster and faster, human beings still seemed to need a way of putting all that swooshing and whoosh-ing into a restful perspective. So when Americans wanted to say something was moving too fast — even in those speedy times — for even them to conceive of, they would say, as those of us over 50 can remember, it's moving "at the speed of light."

The speed of light. Now that was getting serious. The speed of light, as we learned in school, is 186,000 miles per second. And those of us who stayed in school long enough soon learned that what was true of visible light was also true of electromagnetic radiation in general.

In short, the speed of light served the folks of 40 years ago as a reassurance. At a time when many people were having their doubts about traditional religion, it told them that there was still a realm so amazing that it could be called, and thought of as, god-like. The immensity of outer space could be summed up with the observation that it took starlight millions and billions light years to reach our planet traveling at 186,000 miles per second. How could you possi-bly beat that? Why, even if our own sun suddenly went out, we wouldn't know it for eight minutes.

So, went the implied moral, we might be moving faster and faster in our everyday lives, but when we compared our actual pace with the speed of light, we were almost sitting still. From our perspective 40 years later, we can look back and say that the people of that time, including our younger selves, had chosen the electronic side of life to serve as their vision of the unattainable. Yet, as we all have learned, ideas have a funny way of producing side effects, some-times unintended, at others unforeseen. The unintended effect of the electronic view of life was that the unattainable speed of light

made it possible for human beings to rationalize the fact they were on vacation, spending hours lying on a big towel on the beach. So if they hadn't had a brand-new idea in almost an hour, they could feel less guilty since they were only joining their fellow humans in a fit of relaxation.

That was the unintended side effect. The unforeseen effect is one we see too often. The electronic side of life now accounts for much of the news in the business sections and magazines. Dagwood Bumstead and Mary Worth, two old comic strip heroes, are computerized because they reflect a world in which you can sometimes get all your business done sitting in front of a computer even in your bedroom and neatly attired in your bathrobe. No matter what time of day — at work or in the middle of a sleepless night — you can log on, point, click, and see how your shares on the Tajikistan Stock Exchange are doing or learn that police in a small village near Manchester are beginning to treat yesterday's strange death as a murder. Meanwhile, what I'll call the rhetoric of the business world has shifted from the old notion of working one's normal hours, say nine to five, to one where normal hours means 24 hours, period.

You know it as well as I do. As our personal and business lives become increasingly electronic — as the speed of light becomes finally the *attainable* — we are running some serious physical and mental risks. The idea of *rest* has become controversial. Rest is something you routinely deny in order to keep up with the times, with business, with the news, with the next big thing. Sleep, in its turn, is an old-fashioned bad habit you engage in during your off-hours. And should you stretch out in your office for a few minutes of ... please forgive my bad taste ... *doing nothing*, some pop-up or synthesized voice from your computer will tell you have just received e-mail from Singapore or Moscow or Montevideo or, for all I know, the dark side of the moon. At the speed of light.

When the speed of light still seemed unattainable or even god-like 40 years ago, it helped us to control a particular human anxiety: the fear that life was becoming inhuman. The atom bomb had already taught us that the world was beyond our control and beyond our means of self-protection. Run as fast as you could, hop in a cab and tell the driver to drive as fast as he could, you still couldn't outrun the heat, the fire, and the radiation. Bad enough. But imagine how people of that simpler age would respond to the notion, current today, of electronic or data warfare. Never mind waiting for the sound of an explosion: there is none. Never mind running: you can't. An enemy attack now can wipe out the computers that control the electrical power grid, the waterworks, the traffic lights, the Federal government, and the telephones you would have used to call up a cab. The right keyboard strokes and a nasty turn of mind bring everything to a stop. Science fiction 40 years ago. Not today.

Yes, we are in the middle of an electronic revolution. Yes, it is turning human life into a speeding bullet, the exact location of which we are always trying to determine. Exactly how our computers are affecting our minds is a common subject in our magazines and newspapers — and of course on Internet bulletin boards and in chat rooms. Much of it tends to be pie in the sky, and much of it looks at electronic technology as a divine dispenser of whiz-bang gizmos that are praised because they are cool, not because anyone needs them or wants them. And a lot of the talk and writing about electronic devices is pessimistic or plain glum. Did I really buy opera tickets so some buffoon's pager could go off in the middle of *The Marriage of Figaro*? Do I really want to hear a girl breaking up with her boyfriend on her cell phone in the middle of the street — and know exactly why she thinks he's a jerk?

But I wonder if there might be a way of looking at our electronic age that is both less whiz-bang and less glum. Is there some way of looking at all these cables and clever machines — each of which will be upgraded within a few hours of our paying money to buy it — that might actually leave us with a smile?

We might start with considering icons. And no, I don't mean those cute little graphics on a computer screen that you click on. I mean real icons. In our culture, which always surrounds us with images, now increasingly electronic, we might consider how much our images resemble the icons that earlier cultures worshiped. I have

in mind the cultures of the Eastern churches, in Greece, Byzantium, and Russia.

Icons were single images, most usually of Christ or the Virgin, but also of saints. They were used — and I mean used, not simply looked at — with a purpose, that being to focus the worshiper on the holy being and his or her significance. Most important of all, icons were static: they did not show Christian drama, whether the harrowing of hell or the raising of Lazarus. They usually showed the holy face, less often the whole body. Not necessarily in repose, but in one caught static moment.

Is it outrageous, in the age of computer icons, to suggest that we could be living in a new iconic age? Of contemplative icons? Images out of old movies have a power over our souls that is testified to by posters sold in every gift shop in America. What if, in the middle of the night when you can't get to sleep, you conjure up a modern icon to soothe your soul in your quest for universal values? It could be James Dean leaning on his Porsche. Ingrid Bergman saying, "Play it, Sam." It could be Babe Ruth pointing at the stands. It could be a private image you carry around in a secret part of your brain. Why not?

I jest, but not completely. In the midst of an iconic age, whether in mediaeval Russia or the modern United States, thinking with *art* takes us farther than thinking only with *words*. Images seem to have infinite meanings for us. The richest companies in the world spend some of their wealth on logos they hope will be meaningful. In the contemplative setting of the supermarket, the power of images is confirmed by the booming sales in branded packaged goods.

We respond to images. The corporate logo, the mediaeval icon, and the movie star's face are, of course, not the same. But they all speak to us somehow. And once we admit the power that modern icons — Marilyn Monroe or Mickey Mantle — have over our minds and once we also sense the powerful revival all around us of religious and spiritual feelings, it is awfully tempting to conclude that we are living in an age of faith. Why, we even have relics. Not the bones of

saints, but the jewelry of Jackie. Yet stars and saints have much in common, including the golden aura around their faces and bodies that is real or merely perceived by those who adore them. Movie theatres are called contemplative places, at least when some movies are showing. The same is true of museums: you notice how hushed they are, that no one laughs? We are too involved with the images to laugh. We are busy not being busy.

If the electronic revolution has speeded up our lives to an extent I find dismaying, it is good news that our lives at the same time have become more visual. I hasten to add that it is not *always* good. As every newspaper, Web site, magazine, TV show, and billboard is trying to zonk its messages straight into our eyeballs, we find that schools have trouble with kids who don't — or can't — think with words any more. We have children, and adults, who take the image for the thing portrayed by the image — yet art and contemplation are not skin deep. Perhaps the schools and the colleges will have to consider visual literacy, the ability to see images for what they truly are, and to teach how to discriminate among images as we teach how to discriminate among words and numbers.

But the richness and variety of the images around us and our habit of absorbing them can do us some good. If in our curious world the *average* speed seems to be the speed of light, I believe we can use good images as icons — as objects of religious veneration if that is what one wants — but more as objects of contemplation and thought — as objects to slow us down. I noted before that Eastern religious icons are static, not dramatic. They require anyone looking at them to supply the drama, the script, the movement, the thought.

We may have no choice about the speed of the world in which we go about our lives and businesses. Few of us are constituted to be monks or hermits or even Thoreau: the cabin in the woods is too lonely, and life in it is too hard for most of us. We may have to get on with our lives, running as fast as we can just to stay in place, spinning like dervishes, speeding like bullets. But at the same time, the richness of our physical and mental archives of images should allow us to seize upon images that somehow speak to us, that somehow comfort

us, that somehow show us who we are ... or who we could become. And perhaps these images, these static icons to which I have referred, can refresh us from the rigors of days, and often nights, spent moving at the speed of light.

Town and Gown:
A Capital Case

IT IS IMPOSSIBLE, at least for me, to imagine Cambridge without Harvard, New York without Columbia, and most certainly the District of Columbia without The George Washington University. It also is implausible to imagine Harvard without Cambridge, Columbia without New York, and GW without the District. The cities and the universities in question, and many others, belong to each other. The universities are in the cities, but they are most decidedly *of* their cities as well.

This inseparable relationship has been evident since the found · ing of the universities, yet there has been an odd gap in the relation- ship. While American schools have always recognized and even proclaimed their sense of duty to the nation, they have been rather less straightforward about proclaiming, never mind extending, a sense of civic duty toward their own neighborhoods. This civic sense, to the extent that it exists at all, is only some 30 years old. It is a matter of history that the earliest insistence on responsibility for the local community came from the political — mainly student — radi- cals of the 1960s rather than from more established forces.

Speech to the American Council on Education's 81st Annual Meeting at a panel entitled "Higher Education and Civic Responsibility: A Capital Case Study," February 15, 1999

A friend once characterized the conditions that led to this state of affairs as the elite position the university had toward the town. He said about the time just before student activity turned radical: "The only time that the students and the working class ever got together is when a town cop whacked an undergraduate over the head when a keg party took to the streets." When the radicals took to the streets, that changed.

In 1988, when I became president of GW, radicalism had faded from campus and was no longer the motive for concern for the well being of the District of Columbia. The more current and compelling motive was the need to anchor GW more firmly within its home city. This motive combined charitable impulses with a note of political and social realism.

We had come to understand that belonging to Washington as Washington belonged to us was not merely an image or a passing reference to the landscape. The mutual dependency was all around us, from services and utilities to, especially, most of our workforce. Could we look at the children of those who staffed the University — could we look at their educational and social needs — and think of them as mere "Colonial adjuncts?" (Colonials being the name of GW's sports teams.)

We could not. So early in the 1990s we announced a major scholarship program for graduates of the District's high schools, funded with $7 million. The realism of this project is obvious. But the scholarship program had a symbolic value as well in that it helped to break down the invisible, but real, barrier that until then seemed to separate GW from the city where it had first settled and has continued to grow.

I can also testify that, having taken that dramatic step, it became routine for GW to be, and to stay, in touch with municipal government and to further cooperation. Even during Washington's series of crises in the 1990s, the continuing contact never ceased.

It would be pleasing to say that what GW began doing less than 10 years ago was a reaffirmation, or a new expression, of older traditions.

But that was not the case. Like many other urban universities, town-gown relations were chilly, infrequent, or matters for the law, as the story about the cop and the drunken student I referred to illustrates. And as for tradition, this kind of relationship dates to the 12th and 13th centuries when the first great European universities were founded. Much as schools are famous for their traditions, this was one we could do without.

In fact, we could replace it with a new and apt recognition of the relationship between higher education and economic development. What Washington needed, it seemed to us, were the talented graduates of the city's high schools no more and no less than the talented graduates of schools from all across the country and, indeed, the world. You'll notice I said *What Washington needed*, not *What GW needed*. We could fill our classrooms, no matter. But what Washington needed was for its high school graduates to become college graduates and the holders of graduate degrees.

These were people who knew their city and understood its needs from the ground up. Now they had to have the opportunity to develop the skills that would put their knowledge to daily use. Whatever the particular use, it would enable a rising generation of Washingtonians to be involved in the life of their city, in government or out, and to earn good salaries while they did so.

And so promising were the results of our original scholarship program that we soon added many other efforts aimed at the well being of the District of Columbia. Take my word for it: Many of these programs were started and staffed by GW students whose introduction to civic consciousness and duty became central to their academic experience.[2]

This, of course, sounds like simply a local answer to a local question. And so it is, in part. Washington is not Cambridge or New York, so the opportunities and the problems facing us are different from those facing Harvard or Columbia. But I think what we have

[2] For anyone interested in learning about the scope and operation of these programs, the information is available from GW's Office of University Relations at (202) 994-6460.

done by improving our relationship with the city of Washington has national significance. I believe so because I also believe we are now in the middle of an episode in which American universities are being recognized — by others *and* by themselves — as major resources for the re-creation of American society.

As evidence for this proposition, I will quote to you from an essay by Evan Dobelle, president of Trinity College in Hartford, and Bruce Katz called "Higher Education: U.S. Cities' Untapped Assets."

"Bound by history and economic reality to their respective cities, these institutions are uniquely positioned to spur community revival." They continue, saying, "Schools located in stressed neighborhoods cannot wall off problems. Neighborhood decline will eventually breach the barriers. An institution in an unsafe or merely unpleasant area will lose some prospective students and faculty members. And unlike private firms, universities and colleges generally cannot afford to rebuild their specialized facilities in a new part of town, particularly if high crime and low investment have reduced the value of their existing properties."

A strong realistic statement. But I want to advance an even larger proposition than the one put forth by Dobelle and Katz: That by virtue of their locations in the heart of America's domestic crisis, our urban universities hold in their hands an important spiritual key to our national future.

In a quiet but steady way, we have been living through an historic meeting of the minds of American business and the American academy. We may roughly date its beginning to the late 1980s when President George Bush's education advisers, nearly all of them corporate executives, began talking about the deficits in American education. It has become increasingly clear ever since that lessons taught in our schools directly connect with this nation's productivity, including most especially its technological drive. College and university graduates form the staff, if you will, of the country's economic dominance.

We have an extraordinary and pervasive system of education — even though it is decentralized and formally not a system at all. It ranges from the nearby community college to the universities recognized everywhere in the world as truly great. Movements among the many parts of this system — by students transferring or seeking additional degrees at different schools and by faculty seeking employment and tenure — has created what I like to call "The University of the United States." It is an organism of education the likes of which the world has never seen before. Countries that seek to emulate us or compete with us are having to learn from our national higher education system.

And I come back to this: This system supports American industry and business from the local manufacturer to the largest multinational corporation. It is, therefore, inconceivable that schools so tied to our national and international economies should not make their communities part of the process. I will take it a step further and say institutions of higher learning, like other institutions, have to *make sense* as well as *teach sense*. I believe profoundly that those who work in higher education hold the American future in their hands.

And I ask you please not to dismiss what I am saying as "vocationalism." Universities are not chasing Homer and Dante and Shakespeare off campus. The business departments have not seized the classrooms and the budgets of the English departments. The philosophy department has not been ridden out of town on a rail. To the contrary, consider how the traditional subjects are gaining renewed interest and status because they connect with so many activities of what I call our "college society." We want to turn out educated men and women, people who know how to learn and who may well learn about Athenian history, mediaeval cathedrals, or Victorian novels through the most up-to-date of our media and methods.

At the same time, our advances in information technology continue to make their way in two directions at once. First, from our schools out to the nation and then, second, from the hands-on professionals of our nation, who live nearby, into our colleges and universities. Indeed, GW's offerings in law, business, and foreign

affairs, for example, are enriched because we draw adjuncts from our neighbors who do law, business, and foreign affairs for a living.

What all this suggests is that the chemistry between our schools and our neighborhoods must become one of the triumphs of America in the new century — in fact, a triumph that fuels other triumphs in business, social relations, spiritual renewal. The people who will produce this triumph are, at least some of them, our neighbors. We cannot, we dare not, ignore their talents. And if these triumphs do not materialize, will we truly feel shocked to learn that what kept them away was our inability to turn the cities from problems into assets?

We cannot export our problems or ourselves. We can't escape to the suburbs or retreat into gated communities. Just so, we cannot export our assets, either. We can't let the potential of talented young people lie unused or go far away when they are needed here. I began by saying I cannot imagine GW without Washington. Let me amend that. I cannot imagine GW — not a robust, healthy GW — without Washingtonians.

The Education Society
and the Public Schools

My child's success and happiness in life
will be determined by my child's education.

I TAKE THIS PROPOSITION to be self-evident and inarguable. I
doubt there is an American parent who does not believe this simple
and straightforward statement. I doubt there is an American, child-
less or with grown children, who would not agree. We have become
an education society, a society that places great expectation on
schooling because it has great faith in the promises education holds.

All to the good, you might think. But as educators, the providers of
a universally acknowledged and admired service, you know that anyone
and everyone is telling you your business — telling you how to teach
better, demanding that you account for everything you do, or throwing
on your desk the latest proposals for even better public education.

This is not easy, and I have no guaranteed solution to the problems
of public education. But I do want to offer you a broad perspective with
some small and specific suggestions, a useful combination, I hope. And
I will begin by saying that our public schools are experiencing two

Speech to the National School Board Association's Leadership Conference, January 28, 2001

phenomena that our universities also are experiencing, so I know something about them firsthand. I call them *competition* and *spillage*.

Educational competition has been around since the first schools opened their doors — or rather convened in a Greek olive grove a few millennia ago. In my lifetime, schools certainly had to cope with what students learned in the public library or read in a magazine or heard from their parents. In an education society, where everyone is trying to build up a portfolio of information and, we hope, knowledge, schools can't make their students take a pledge that says, "I promise not to learn anything outside school." So, competition is not new, nor undesirable. But today it mainly boils down to the Internet.

From kindergarten through graduate school, schools are wrestling with Internet competition. Sometimes, the Internet is an alternative or merely a supplemental information provider, not more "competitive" than the encyclopedia on the public library's shelves. Sometimes, however, the competition is more direct. Some school or university or private company is offering courses online, by mail, or on video that duplicates what your school is teaching on an actual attendance basis. And the Web is full of providers who would like to take over what they believe your school doesn't know how to do — and, naturally, do it for less, whether it is teaching basic grammar or advanced cuneiform.

Universities are already facing this direct competition, and the public schools will be facing it soon enough. Certainly, the challenges of charter schools have let any public educator know that there are means for competing with the schoolhouse. The Internet is an obvious means with a lot of support. Let me remind you that just two days after his inauguration, President George W. Bush said he wanted to seek federal subsidies to help the poor buy computers and connect to the Internet in order to narrow the digital divide. In other words, the new Republican administration is following the previous Democratic administration in continuing to pay tribute to the Internet as the key to becoming *really* smart. So, it's going to become educational doctrine. And school boards that are not thinking carefully about how to use the Internet are school boards that are going to be very severely shocked.

Allied with competition is what I call "spillage" — the tendency in our education society to allow, and even expect, people to learn things earlier or later than what used to be the norm. It is here now, and it is a phenomenon with a future. We see it clearly in the admissions office of any college. There are high school seniors who appear with the expected courses. There are some with not quite what they should have among the standard courses, but with other unexpected things in their portfolios. And there are still others who appear with loads of advanced credits. These last are students who have already taken college-level courses. They are especially interesting to admissions deans for what they already know and also for what their learning testifies to — namely, a lot of spunk, smarts, and initiative.

Once every child, even the poorest, has a computer and access to the Internet — that old devil, the public library, will probably be the locus of computer access — that child will be free to start doing the kind of work our public schools once believed only they were licensed to do. And when that happens, the schools will have to do many things.

First, they will have to ascertain what the child has learned — and whether the learning is good and factual. By way of an aside, I will remind you of something you all know: The Internet is full of remarkable information and knowledge, but full of fiction and rumor masquerading as wisdom, too.

Second, the schools will have to figure out how such a child, and what that child has learned, can be integrated into the established system of learning of the schools. This will be particularly difficult if the schools take no account of Internet learning by youngsters.

Third, any examination of the student will have to stand up to local, legislative, and even constitutional scrutiny.

Integration may be the key word. I do not mean racial integration — a separate issue — but educational integration or even functional integration. In other words, how will the schools integrate the inevitable impact of the Internet, and other educational competitors, with their own programs and missions? How do you make the blackboard lie down with the modem?

To give you a better idea of what I mean, let me give you another example of spillage. Millions of immigrants are coming to the United States without the basic skills that are routinely taught in our schools. Those of you who remember *The Education of Hyman Kaplan* or are the children or grandchildren of immigrants know that they went to evening courses in public schools — or in union halls or factories, but taught usually by public school teachers — to learn English or math. It was a wonderful prize for the immigrants, and should be a point of historic pride for public education.

But *historic* won't do any longer. Going to school at the end of a long work day in our suburbanized society looks implausible today. We, American educators, must devise ways for the immigrant to master English under his or her own roof or transform knowledge of medicine or accountancy acquired in a different language and a different culture into a form that can pass a state licensing exam and be put to good use here. Our schools will have to find ways to serve this market that are lively and up to date as well as educational.

There, I've said it. The magic word — market. The schools are serving an enormous, complicated, demanding, and competitive market. The competition doesn't come only from the charter schools, which I mentioned before, but from private corporations or universities taking over a city's department of education, from the push from more and more private schools, from home schooling. The monopoly is gone, and the market is here to stay. Like any market, it has its regulators — not only city and state legislative committees, but the media and the public in general. Everyone has something to say. Everyone has a stake. Therefore, everyone has a right. Facing competition and regulation makes it sound as if the public schools are a business. In a way, that's exactly what they have become in our education society.

And in a marketplace like this, the schools must look at integrating the Internet, and other tools, into a resource of their own. A recent article in *School Board News*, the publication of this organization, described how a tiny school district in Alaska was using the Internet to reach home schoolers statewide. I hope you read the article.

It's an excellent example, as the article states, of how the Internet tends to "bust down our traditional walls." If the children in this experiment have learned as much as those who actually sat in a classroom, then what arguments remain for building and maintaining bricks-and-mortar schools?

I will offer you two. The first is to be able to say that no one offers better education over the Internet than we do. That means you really have to do so. That means adapting your teaching to the requirements of the Internet. That means devising ways of keeping in touch with children — some of them very young — to foster, not to mention monitor, what they are learning and what they are not learning.

The second argument is just as important, perhaps more so. We talk about school as a socializing experience, and so it is, in the sense of learning to play well with others. But schooling, at all levels, has another social component. Sitting in a classroom with others requires explaining one's point of view and defending it, understanding another's point of view and accepting or rejecting it. This intellectual-social component of education, in my view, is one of the most important things schools do. The information and the knowledge are available and long have been. The Internet, as I began by suggesting, changed the means of acquiring information, but not the desire or the ability to do so. But school rooms, where students at all levels face each other, help to socialize the intellectual development of students. Thus, your second argument should run more or less like this:

"We will bring our Internet students together from time to time so they may engage one another and their teachers. We will use some techniques already available — like threaded conversation and chat rooms — to promote the intellectual-social advances of our students. In other words, we will use the best techniques to overcome isolation and to promote a crystallization of learning."

So much for Doc Trachtenberg's prescription: "Make two arguments and call me in the morning." They are important arguments, and I am sure you know how to make them. But they are not easy — and making them requires a great deal of enthusiasm and spirit.

I am aware of many elements that are affecting spirit, or morale, in public education, but two of them are critical. They are recruitment of new teachers and keeping the politicians and media on your side, or at least at bay. These endeavors have been difficult for you, and will remain so. But these are problems I deal with, so let me offer you some examples and ideas.

Schools tend to think of media people as snoops looking for trouble. But you're in a marketplace now. You *want* media attention, especially when it's free and *positive*. Learn to talk with media folk and provide them with stories they'd like to cover, for example, school debates on current affairs, polls on how kids see sex and drugs in their schools and their lives, the notion that the world owes everyone a computer and a color printer. Watching young minds develop is exciting. Plato knew that and so did John Dewey and Horace Mann and many educators since. The media love excitement. So, let your kids excite them.

One of the best ways to do this is to remind the media, the public, and *yourselves* that public school students aren't units or categories, but young members of the species homo sapiens who tend to be cuter than a button and smarter than a whip. What they think, what they have to say, what they feel are all worth observing and knowing. Teaching must be humane, so let the human faces of your students and teachers be seen far and wide.

Now, problems with recruitment. Your district or state has openings. You advertise them, here and abroad. You put on a job fair. No one shows up, at least no one you'd hire. First, ask yourself, what is the problem? Is it class size? Teaching conditions? The pay? What? It has to be something. And you have to figure out what that something is. When you have, go to those new good friends of yours in the media, tell them you're having a press conference, invite some politicians, and ask loudly what the city or the state is going to do to help you solve your problems. They are *your* problems, remember that. It's fine to have NEA lobbyists beating down the doors on Capitol Hill, but Uncle Sam doesn't solve local problems. You do. You have to learn to lobby.

And because we live in an education society, you have a good chance of getting the media and the politicians on your side. Education is a hot button. Don't be afraid to push it. And don't be afraid to be a bit pushy. I believe those who are always getting ready to meet heavy-metal resistance or competition tend to get less of each than average. Be prepared. Be tough.

And be comforted: You are not alone. At the present time, we are seeing a massive reawakening of interest in teaching in the public schools. You don't have to be a news junkie these days to hear frequent stories about yet another lawyer or Internet mechanic or bigshot executive who has decided that teaching, with its opportunity to nurture, is better than what he or she was doing before, the pay cut notwithstanding.

Welcome these people, and make sure that having the proper credentials does not stand in the way of recruiting someone like this. Be comforted, as I said, that such people want to teach. Keep in mind we have an enormous reservoir of idealism in this country. And certainly teaching requires idealism.

You have to cherish the ideal that children want to learn. You must also cherish the ideal that enabling them to learn is liberating for them and for you. Teaching thrives on challenges because of idealism — they are there to be overcome, not to signal defeat. And idealism is fed by understanding that we have the means, traditional and up to date, to teach and reach practically everyone with practically anything. And that we, with our idealism and our means, are the best people to do the job.

I showed a copy of this speech to a friend before I got here. He has a sense of humor. After finishing, he gasped and said, "You're asking the public schools to stop being villains and become heroes? We only have words to criticize them. Who's going to teach us the whole new vocabulary we'll need to sing their praises? Who could do *that*?"

I told him I thought I knew.

Afterthoughts

THE UNSPEAKABLE TERRORIST ATTACKS of September 11 haunted me during the editing of this book and still do. Others have spoken and written eloquently and movingly about the day and the events, and I have no reason to add anything now, though the force of that calamity remains present and powerful.

A strange byproduct of those assaults was to save GW from what now seems like a very minor calamity — the planned closing of the university because of the expected demonstrations at the meetings of the World Bank and International Monetary Fund. Their buildings happen to be immediately adjacent to our campus, and we reluctantly decided to close for reasons of safety at the urging of the police.

Before September 11, the closing of the school, we all believed on campus, was the worst thing ever to happen to the university and the source of a great deal of debate and even friction. Shortly after September 11, the World Bank and the IMF decided, sensibly, to call off their meetings, and the protesters decided, sensibly and probably politically, not to protest, at least not en masse in our neighborhood. Our great calamity vanished into the rubble of the World Trade Center. I would prefer to have suffered our little calamity than the national one that forestalled ours.

Yet there was also an irony. For the sake of safety, we closed the school the day of the assaults; I hasten to add we also closed for the sake of our grief and as a gesture of respect for the dead and the missing. But safety, in those first fearful minutes and hours, was the first reason for closing. This time, of course, there was no debate or friction.

This irony may add a useful illustration about the life of a university. It can be contentious; universities, as I am often reminded when I venture off campus, are famous for squabbles over small stakes. I think that is unkind. The stakes often seem very large to us and often are. A university president who does not recognize that he has many constituencies with legitimate interests and needs, or who merely sees various factions and cells "squabbling over trivia," will soon be unemployed or be the head of a third-rate (and plummeting toward fourth-rate) institution. But our internal disputes do not really often leave campus, except perhaps in media reports, which amount to little more than gossip-column jibes. More to the point, universities are not consumed with internal strife and not absorbed with the rumblings of their own stomachs. They look outward.

In other words, despite the durability and resilience of phrases like "the ivory tower" and "ivy-covered walls," we are as much a part of the streets, the neighborhood, the nation, and the world as any other public or private or even religious institution. I seriously doubt, having dealt for many years with people in other fields, that our institutional behavior is any more arcane, tolerates any more quarrels, or has any more shibboleths than Exxon or Greenpeace or a synod of bishops. There is no ivory and not that much ivy on campus.

The perceived threat of demonstrations at the World Bank and the actual attacks on the World Trade Center and the Pentagon bring this point home. Neither had anything to do with my campus, or any other, directly. In the first case, the problems we foresaw were a matter of physical proximity that was in turn simply a matter of happenstance; in the second, our horror was a matter of national proximity, a sense that an assault on our nation was an assault on each of us, as individual human beings and as institutions.

In several of the speeches collected here, I refer to our sense of national proximity most often in terms of the connection between the rise and expansion of the American economy after World War II and the rise and expansion of America's universities and the influence of university graduates. I do not abandon that idea now, but I think I clearly need to broaden it by giving other kinds of connections fuller thought and treatment.

Events outside our libraries, laboratories, and classrooms direct us and shape us and guide us in the academy even more than our internal deliberations or pernicious so-called squabbles. Our connections are not exclusively economic nor a feeder industry to business and government. They are social, moral, and emotional in addition to being educational and intellectual. That is the point, I confess now, that I wish I had developed in some of these speeches. Universities, or more frequently experts on university faculties, may often act as gadflies and critics, and to some their role seems to be institutionalized, even predictable, sniping from a safe distance. That is not really so, for one could say the same of the press, the lobbies and non-profit organizations, the Republican and Democratic parties, the unions, the think tanks, the churches, the activists of varying political stripes, racial organizations, and probably any institution I could name. Like them, universities help to guide and shape our society just as much as the rest of our society guides and shapes its various institutions. There is no "safe distance."

In that sense, a university is simply part of the American landscape, to me a critical part; if I did not believe that, I would not have devoted nearly all of my working life to university governance. But I did so, and continue to do so, with an understanding that my own particular enthusiasms and passions are matched by the equal enthusiasms and passions of other people in other lines of work. We all think our institutions are critical and believe optimistically in their growth, and we are probably all correct.

So let me suggest that it might be better to think of America as a mosaic rather than a landscape, as a man-made work, even a work of art — but a mosaic for the age of computers, not the age of

Byzantium, a *virtual* mosaic. In the virtual mosaic, like the classical one, each piece is important to making the whole picture, but each part is dynamic, capable of changing shape and growing, rather than cut to size and cemented in place forever. And the most amazing thing about our virtual mosaic is that the growth of one part — of one institution or individual or class or race — need not distort or degrade or displace any other part. The whole picture changes and grows as each of its institutions and citizens changes and grows.

It's an idea to conjure with. I plan to.

About the Author

S TEPHEN J OEL T RACHTENBERG became the 15th president of The George Washington University on August 1, 1988. He came to GW from the University of Hartford (Conn.), where he had been President for 11 years. Before assuming the presidency of Hartford, Trachtenberg served for eight years at Boston University as Vice President for Academic Services and Academic Dean of the College of Liberal Arts. Earlier, in Washington, D.C., he was a Special Assistant for two years to the U.S. Education Commissioner,

Department of Health, Education and Welfare. He has been an attorney with the U.S. Atomic Energy Commission and a legislative aide to former Indiana Congressman John Brademas.

A Professor of Public Administration, he published *Thinking Out Loud* (American Council on Education Oryx Press, 1998) and *Speaking His Mind* (American Council on Education Oryx Press, 1994), collections of his essays on the state of higher education. He is co-editor of the book *The Art of Hiring in America's Colleges & Universities* (Prometheus Books, 1993). He authored chapters in the books *Academic Leaders as Managers* (Jossey-Bass, 1982), *Leaders on Leadership: The College Presidency* (Jossey-Bass, 1988), and *Productivity & Higher Education* (Peterson's Guide, 1992). His articles have appeared in publications such as *The Educational Record*, *Phi Delta Kappan*, *The Association of Governing Boards of Universities and Colleges AGB Reports*, *Resources in Education*, *Journal for Higher Education Management*, *The College Board Review*, *The College Marketing Alert*, *The Chronicle of Higher Education*, *The Washington Post*, and *The New York Times*. Trachtenberg also has served as a consulting editor to *The Journal of Education* and *The Presidency*.

He currently serves on the boards of the Greater Washington Board of Trade, the Urban League of Greater Washington, the D.C. Federal City Council, and Riggs Bank. He has been appointed by the city's Mayor to serve on the District of Columbia Tax Revision Commission, as well as the District of Columbia Committee to Promote Washington. He serves on the boards of the Chief of Naval Operations (CNO) Executive Panel and the International Association of University Presidents. He currently chairs the Maryland/D.C. State Committee of Selection competition for the Rhodes Scholarships. He is a member of the Council on Foreign Relations. Trachtenberg also serves as a trustee of Al-Akhawayn University in Morocco. He has served as president of the American Association of University Administrators. In 1988, he was elected to the National Collegiate Athletic Association (NCAA) Presidents Commission.

In 2001, Southern Connecticut State University awarded Trachtenberg with an Honorary Doctor of Laws degree. He was named a "Washingtonian of the Year 2000" in the January 2001

issue of *Washingtonian* magazine. In June 2000, King Mohammed VI of Morocco decorated him as a "Grand Officier Du Wissam Al Alaoui." Also in 2000, he was awarded the Order of St. John of Jerusalem, Knight Grand Cross for Distinguished Service to Freemasonry and Humanity. In 1999, both Gratz College and Boston University awarded him an Honorary Doctor of Humane Letters degrees. He received the Jewish National Fund 1999 "Tree of Life" award. That same year, by proclamation of the City and County of San Francisco, February 2, 1999, was proclaimed "Stephen Joel Trachtenberg Day in San Francisco." Similarly, by resolution of the Council of the District of Columbia, January 22, 1998, was declared "Stephen Joel Trachtenberg Day" in honor of Trachtenberg's commitment to minority students, scholarship programs, public school partnerships, and community service.

In 1997, he received the U.S. Department of State Secretary's Open Forum Distinguished Public Service Award, an Honorary Doctor of Laws degree from Mount Vernon College, and the Grand Cross — the highest honor of the Scottish Rite of Freemasonry; a portrait of him was dedicated and placed in the Hall of Honor at the House of the Temple. In 1996, the Odessa State Medical University (Ukraine) awarded Trachtenberg the Honorary Doctor of Medicine degree, and the American Association of University Administrators presented him with the 1996 Distinguished Service Award. That same year he also received the 1996 B'nai B'rith Humanitarian Award.

In 1995, Trachtenberg was awarded an Honorary Doctor of Laws degree by Richmond College (London) and the John Jay Award for Outstanding Professional Achievement by Columbia University, as well as the 1995 Newcomen Society Award. The American Jewish Congress also honored him with its 1995 Spirit of Democracy Award. In 1994, Trachtenberg received an Honorary Doctor of Public Administration degree from South Korea's Kyonggi University. In 1993, the Washington, D.C. Urban League named him "Father of the Year." He received the International Salute Award in honor of Martin Luther King, Jr., and the Hannah G. Solomon Award from the National Council of Jewish Women in

1992. And, in 1990, Hanyang University in Korea awarded him an Honorary Doctor of Laws, and Kyung Hee University in Korea presented him with the University Medal of Highest Honor.

Trachtenberg received an Honorary Doctor of Humanities degree from the University of Hartford (Conn.) in 1989. In 1988, the Connecticut Bar Association honored him with its Distinguished Public Service Award, and he was recognized by the Hartford NAACP for his contributions to the education of minority students. He received a 1987 Human Relations Award from the National Conference of Christians and Jews. In 1986, Trinity College (Conn.) awarded him an Honorary Doctor of Humane Letters degree. In 1984, he was presented The Mt. Scopus Award from Hebrew University in Jerusalem, and in 1982 he was celebrated by the Connecticut Region of Hadassah with the Myrtle Wreath Award. Four years earlier, in 1978, Trachtenberg was named one of the Top 100 Leaders in the American Academy in a *Change* magazine poll.

Trachtenberg earned the B.A. degree from Columbia University in 1959, the J.D. from Yale University in 1962 and the Master of Public Administration from Harvard University in 1966. In 1968, he was selected as a Winston Churchill Traveling Fellow for study in Oxford, England. He is a member of Phi Beta Kappa. Trachtenberg and his wife, Francine Zorn Trachtenberg, have two children: Adam Maccabee, B.A. from Columbia University in 1997; and Ben Lev, B.A. from Yale University in 2001. Mrs. Trachtenberg is senior vice president at WETA, Washington, D.C.'s public television station.